ATD Soft Skills Series

Creativity
in Talent Development

Donna Porter and
Nancy Tennant

atd
PRESS

Alexandria, VA

ATD Press is an internationally renowned source of insightful and practical information
on talent development, training, and professional development.

ATD Press
1640 King Street
Alexandria, VA 22314 USA

Ordering information: Books published by ATD Press can be purchased by visiting ATD's
website at td.org/books or by calling 800.628.2783 or 703.683.8100.

Library of Congress Control Number: 2021943944

ISBN-10: 1-952157-60-9
ISBN-13: 978-1-952157-60-8
e-ISBN: 978-1-952157-61-5

ATD Press Editorial Staff
Director: Sarah Halgas
Manager: Melissa Jones
Content Manager, Career Development: Lisa Spinelli
Developmental Editor: Jack Harlow
Text Design: Shirley E.M. Raybuck
Cover Design: John Anderson Jr.

Creativity Journal Graphics by Gwen Frederickson, Just Gwen Designs

Printed by BR Printers, San Jose, CA

To Mom and Dad
Thank you for answering God's call
to adopt me and for loving me
until the ends of the earth.
—DONNA

To CocoBean
My precious tiny dancer
who now dances in my dreams.
—NANCY

To Gwen
THANK YOU to this graphic guru!
Because of you, our vision has been given
arms, legs, eyes, ears, humor, and LIFE!

Contents

About the Series

The world of work is changing. As companies once prioritized radical workplace performance and productivity improvements, they focused on training their employees with the purpose of getting more work done faster. But companies have learned that while their people might be increasingly productive, they aren't working better, particularly with each other. Lurking on the horizon is always greater automation, which will continue to shift the balance between the needs for hard and soft skills. Employees of the future will spend more time on activities that machines are less capable of, such as managing people, applying expertise, and communicating with others. More than ever, soft skills are being recognized as a premium.

Enter talent development.

TD professionals play a unique role in addressing the increasing demand for soft skills. They work with people and on behalf of people: A trainer facilitating a group of learners. A team of instructional designers working cross-functionally to address a business need. A learning manager using influence to make the case for increased budget or resources. But how can TD professionals expect to develop future employees in these soft skills if they're not developing their own?

At the Association for Talent Development (ATD), we're dedicated to creating a world that works better and empowering TD professionals like you to develop talent in the workplace. As part of this effort, ATD developed the Talent Development Capability Model, a framework to guide the TD profession in what practitioners need to know and do to develop themselves, others, and their organizations. While soft skills appear most prominently under the Building Personal Capability domain, these crucial skills cross every capability in the model, including those under Developing Professional Capability and Impacting Organizational Capability. Soft skills enable TD professionals to take their instructional design, training delivery and facilitation, future readiness, change management, and other TD capabilities to the next level.

Just as TD professionals need resources on how to develop talent, they need guidance in improving their interpersonal and intrapersonal skills—to be more adaptable, self-aware and empathetic, creative, team-oriented and collaborative, and influential and persuasive. This ATD series provides such guidance.

Organized with two parts, each book in the ATD Soft Skills Series tackles one soft skill that TD professionals need to foster in themselves to help the people and organizations they serve. Part 1 breaks down the skill into what it is, why it's important, and the internal or external barriers to improving it. Part 2 turns the lens on the daily work of TD professionals and how they can practice and perfect that skill on the job. Featuring worksheets, self-reflection exercises, and best practices, these books will empower TD professionals to build career resiliency by matching their technical expertise with newfound soft skill abilities.

Books in the series:
- *Adaptability in Talent Development*
- *Emotional Intelligence in Talent Development*
- *Creativity in Talent Development*
- *Teamwork in Talent Development*
- *Influence in Talent Development*

We're happy to bring you the ATD Soft Skills Series and hope these books support you in your future learning and development.

Jack Harlow, Series Editor
Senior Developmental Editor, ATD Press

Series Foreword

Oh, Those Misnamed Soft Skills!

For years organizations have ignored soft skills and emphasized technical skills, often underestimating the value of working as a team, communicating effectively, using problem solving skills, and managing conflict. New managers have failed because their promotions are often based on technical qualifications rather than the soft skills that foster relationships and encourage teamwork. Trainers as recently as a dozen years ago were reluctant to say that they facilitated soft skills training. Why?

Soft Skills: The Past and Now

The reluctance to admit to delivering (or requiring) soft skills often starts with the unfortunate name, "soft," which causes people to view them as less valuable than "hard" skills such as accounting or engineering. The name suggests they are easy to master or too squishy to prioritize developing. On both counts that's wrong. They aren't. In fact, Seth Godin calls them "real" skills, as in, "Real because they work, because they're at the heart of what we need today" (Godin 2017).

Yet, as a society, we seem to value technical skills over interpersonal skills. We tend to admire the scientists who discovered the vaccine for COVID-19 over leaders who used their communication skills to engage the workforce when they were quarantined at home. We easily admit to not knowing how to fly an airplane but readily believe we are creative or can adapt on the fly. We think that because we've been listening all our lives, we are proficient at it—when we're not. As a result, we put much more emphasis on developing our technical skills through advanced degrees and post–higher education training or certifications to land that first or next job than we do on mastering our interpersonal and intrapersonal skills.

Fortunately, many businesses and their leaders are now recognizing the value of having a workforce that has technical knowledge supported by soft skills. That's good because soft skills matter more to your career than you may envision. Consider: as a part of the Jobs Reset Summit, the World Economic Forum determined that 50 percent of the workforce needed reskilling and upskilling. The summit also identified the top 10 job reskilling needs for the future. Eight of the 10 required skills in the 21st century are nontechnical; these skills include creativity, originality, and initiative; leadership and social influence; and resilience, stress tolerance, and flexibility (Whiting 2020). LinkedIn's 2019 *Global Talent Trends Report* showed that acquiring soft skills is the most important trend fueling the future of the workplace: 91 percent of the respondents said that soft skills matter as much or more than technical skills and 80 percent believed they were critical to organizational success (Chandler 2019). A Deloitte report (2017) suggested that "soft skill–intensive occupations will account for two-thirds of all jobs by 2030" and that employees who practice skills associated with collaboration, teamwork, and innovation may be worth $2,000 more per year to businesses. As the cost of robots decreases and AI improves, soft skills like teamwork, problem solving, creativity, and influence will become more important.

Soft skills may not be as optional as one might originally imagine.

Soft Skills: Their Importance

Soft skills are sometimes referred to as enterprise skills or employability skills. Despite their bad rap, they are particularly valuable because they are transferable between jobs, careers, departments, and even industries, unlike hard or technical skills, which are usually relevant only to specific jobs. Communication often lands at the top of the soft skill list, but the category encompasses other skills, such as those included in the ATD Soft Skills Series: emotional intelligence, adaptability, teamwork, creativity, and influence. These personal attributes influence how well employees build trust, establish accountability, and demonstrate professional ethics.

Soft skills are also important because almost every job requires employees to interact with others. Organizations require a workforce that has technical skills and formal qualifications for each job; however, the truth is that business is about relationships. And, organizations depend on relationships to be successful. This is where successful employees, productive organizations, and soft skills collide.

Soft Skills and the Talent Development Capability Model

Talent development professionals are essential links to ensure that organizations have all the technical and soft skills that are required for success. I sometimes get exhausted just thinking about everything we need to know to ensure success for our organizations, customers, leaders, learners, and ourselves. The TD profession is no cookie-cutter job. Every day is different; every design is different; every delivery is different; and every participant is different. We are lucky to have these differences because these broad requirements challenge us to grow and develop.

As TD professionals, we've always known that soft skills are critical for the workforce we're responsible for training and developing. But what about yourself as a TD professional? What soft skills do you require to be effective and successful in your career? Have you ever thought about all the skills in which you need to be proficient?

ATD's Talent Development Capability Model helps you define what technical skills you need to improve, but you need to look beyond the short capability statements to understand the soft skills required to support each (you can find the complete model on page 59). Let's examine a few examples where soft skills are required in each of the domains.

- **Building Personal Capability** is dedicated to soft skills, although all soft skills may not be called out. It's clear that communication, emotional intelligence, decision making, collaboration, cultural awareness, ethical behavior, and lifelong learning are soft skills.

Project management may be more technical, but you can't have a successful project without great communication and teamwork.

- **Developing Professional Capability** requires soft skills throughout. Could instructional design, delivery, and facilitation exist without creativity? You can't coach or attend to career development without paying attention to emotional intelligence (EI) and influence. Even technology application and knowledge management require TD professionals to be adaptable, creative, and team players for success.

- **Impacting Organizational Capability** focuses on the soft skills you'll use while working at the leadership and organizational level. For you to have business insight, be a partner with management, and develop organizational culture, you will need to build teamwork with the C-suite, practice influencing, and use your EI skills to communicate with them. Working on a talent strategy will require adaptability and influence. And you can't have successful change without excellent communication, EI, and teamwork. Future readiness is going to require creativity and innovation.

Simply put, soft skills are the attributes that enable TD professionals to interact effectively with others to achieve the 23 capabilities that span the spectrum of disciplines in the Capability Model.

Soft Skills: The Key to Professionalism

So, as TD professionals we need to be proficient in almost all soft skills to fulfill the most basic responsibilities of the job. However, there's something even more foundational to the importance of developing our soft skills: Only once we've mastered these skills can we project the professionalism that will garner respect from our stakeholders, our learners, and our peers. We must be *professional*, or why else are we called *TD professionals?*

Professionalism is the driving force to advance our careers. To earn the title of TD professional we need to be high performers and exhibit the qualities and skills that go beyond the list of technical TD skills. We need to be soft-skill proficient to deliver services with aplomb. We need to be team members to demonstrate we work well with others. We need to be EI-fluent to ensure that we are aware of, control, and express our emotions and handle interpersonal relationships well. We need to be creative to help our organization achieve a competitive advantage. We need to be adaptable to future-proof our organizations. And we need influencing skills that help us earn that proverbial seat at the table.

We all need role-specific knowledge and skills to perform our jobs, but those who achieve the most are also proficient in soft skills. You will use these skills every day of your life, in just about every interaction you have with others. Soft skills allow you to demonstrate flexibility, resourcefulness, and resilience—and as a result, enhance your professionalism and ensure career success. And a lack of them may just limit your career potential.

Clearly, soft skills are more critical than once thought and for TD professionals and trainers they are likely to be even more critical. Your participants and customers expect you to be on the leading edge of most topics that you deliver. And they also expect you to model the skills required for a successful career. So, which soft skills do you need to become a *professional* TD professional? Is it clearer communication? Interpersonal savvy? Increased flexibility? Self-management? Professional presence? Resourcefulness?

E.E. Cummings said, "It takes courage to grow up and become who you really are." I hope that you have the courage to determine which skills you need to improve to be the best trainer you can be—and especially to identify those misnamed soft skills that aren't *soft* at all. Then establish standards for yourself that are high enough to keep you on your training toes. The five books in the ATD Soft Skills Series offer you a great place to start.

Elaine Biech, Author
Skills for Career Success: Maximizing Your Potential at Work

Introduction

As Asa walks around the room, she points to a drinking glass and says, "frog." In the two-minute exercise, she continues her task as she points to a sticky note and misnames it, "cannibal." As Asa's pace picks up, she traverses the conference room where she finds the usual appointments (whiteboards, flip charts, markers, desks, notebooks, chairs). She rapidly points to each object and proudly misnames it, "cucumber, tall-pine, avocado, chicken, kite, and gullet." Her mood is light; she's enjoying herself. It's funny.

Tim is next—in the same two-minute exercise, under the same instructions. But he's not bouncing around the room like Asa, he's slogging. Tim anxiously looks for an object and then stops dead in his tracks. He tilts his head and waits for a wrong name to surface, but nothing comes. How hard can getting it wrong be, he says under his breath? Just when he thinks he can run out the clock without looking foolish, the instructor says, "Don't stop walking, keep going, keep pointing and misnaming things in the room."

There is nowhere to hide. As Tim gets more frustrated, you can hear the panic grow in his voice. He creates a workaround by using categories of things that can become misnames; he doesn't want to be embarrassed. He decides to start listing animals to get him out of his quandary. Even though the instructor has advised against this, he's desperate. With a little more confidence, we hear "giraffe, aargh . . . antelope, aah . . . elephant, aah, snake, d'oh . . . cat." The instructor says time's up. Tim can't believe how hard this was.

What's Happening?

We are participating in a creativity exercise led by our brilliant friend, Janna Sobel of Second City. In the Name Game, Janna first asks our workshop participants to walk around the room and point to something while quickly saying its name out loud. She tells the participants to keep going until time's up and to get in as many names as they can. Janna gives them two minutes.

In part two of the exercise, Janna asks them to quickly walk around the room, point to something, and this time *misname* it. Again, she encourages participants to get in as many objects as they are able. She again gives them two minutes. That is where we meet Asa, who is creatively and effortlessly misnaming objects, and Tim who is struggling. As most workshop participants learn, it's incredibly hard to misname things when you know the correct name. It's especially hard in the company of your peers. Something in your brain is working on your behalf to save you from embarrassment.

There are four fundamental truths that we learn or relearn as a result of experiencing and extrapolating this simple game to our understanding of creativity:

1. **Creativity is important.** It has various outcomes: to inspire, to communicate, to problem solve, to rise up, to spark innovation, and to persevere. Creativity has been critical to the survival of our species. It's vital today not just on the grand scale of humanity but on a more pedestrian scale. It is important for our jobs, to reach our personal and professional goals, and to thrive and progress in our careers. Creativity is also important in making our lives better, more beautiful, and more meaningful.

2. **Creativity is inside each of us.** Asa is not a misnaming savant and Tim is not creatively challenged. The good news is that science has not decoded a genome sequence that guarantees some people become creative geniuses while the rest of us are creatively barren. We each have the potential to do what Asa has done: unleash the creative that lives inside each of us.

3. **We can learn to be more creative.** There are tools to enable us to become more creative. Is creativity nature or nurture? There is evidence to suggest it is both. We are all born with creativity, but research shows that we lose our creativity as we transition through life. Luckily, nature and nurture are not mutually exclusive. We can learn to be creative, and we can engage underlying processes and tools to become more creative.

4. **We can overcome barriers to creativity.** There are ways to identify and overcome our natural obstacles to creativity. In the Name Game exercise, we see Tim tussle with two barriers to creativity that we will explore later in the book—not wanting to be embarrassed in front of our peers and grabbing for workarounds to restore our confidence in uncertain spaces—which ultimately limit creativity.

Who Should Read This Book?

This book is for anyone who wants to be more creative in their work or personal lives. It is particularly suited to people who work in organizations where creativity is a differentiator with customers, internal and external partners, and other stakeholders. This book offers a "variable reader interface" that meets you where you are in the creative continuum. If you believe that creativity is not in your make-up, this book will help unleash your inner creativity. If you are creative and want to become more creative, this book will nudge you to the next level of creativity. If you are a creative who is looking at that dreaded "blank white page" and no ideas are forthcoming, this book will squeeze you through your bottleneck to open spaces.

Why This Book Matters

We wrote this book with this promise to you: We will deconstruct the morass of information out there on creativity and offer a purposeful and practical way to bring more creativity into your life. We focus on those of you who work in organizations and want to bring creativity to problem solving for customers and employees, especially talent development.

Part 1 of this book sets the foundation by providing context and definition about creativity. We will make the business case for creativity, especially in these tumultuous times. We outline why creativity is essential to organizations and how creativity can be an arrow in your quiver to meet your personal and professional goals. We will also lay bare the myths and wrong assumptions that people have about creativity in organizations. We conclude the first half with three challenges: to bring more creativity to you, your colleagues, and your organization.

In Part 2, we will look at creativity related to talent development roles. We have both held significant talent development roles in large organizations. The Venn diagram intersection of knowing the frontline challenges of these roles and being experts in creativity allows us to offer something unique in this book, building personal capability and competitiveness to create talent opportunities and solve talent problems for your organization. We want to bring creativity into the talent development space. We will offer you tools, techniques, and technologies to become more curious, which is a prerequisite for becoming more creative. This book provides the means to unleash creativity in others, to create an environment where creativity thrives. This can be for the teams you are part of, the groups that you lead, and for your organization as a whole. Finally, we will explore the new world of e-creativity to understand how technology platforms can bring creativity to teams in the virtual spaces we are all inhabiting at an unprecedented pace. We will challenge you to bring creativity to your virtual teams and platforms.

Each chapter offers a practical set of insights, skills, and tools to guide your movement toward your next level of creativity. We will inspire you to use other modalities to bring more creativity to your life. That might be through music, art, novelty hunting, discovery, pop culture, history, intention, and mindfulness. We want you to explore new horizons and go to places you might not usually go.

Create Your Creativity Journal

We recommend you make a creativity journal to use with this book. We will have journal exercises for you to do along the way, and keeping your reactions to them in one place will be beneficial. You'll find a completed creativity journal in the appendix, which you can reference for inspiration and examples. We encourage you to create an multimodal journal, using both words and pictures to express your creativity. We will give you more instructions as you get deeper into the book. Find a new journal, write your name and date inside, and be prepared to amaze yourself, both as you read this book now and years later when you look back at it and say to yourself: *This was when I unlocked the door and released my inner creative into the world.*

Try the Name Game Exercise

Try Janna's Name Game exercise for yourself. You will find that creativity cannot be cultivated by reading about it; you have to demonstrate it, enact it, perform it. Find a group of colleagues. For about two minutes, walk around a room, point at things, and name them correctly. Then walk around the room again and point at new things and misname them. Keep going until two minutes have elapsed. What happened? Put your findings as your first entry in your creativity journal. Draw a picture of what you learned *and* write down your lesson—now you're using your right and left brain to describe what happened.

Becoming More

We are excited to offer new ways for you to embed more creativity into your work and personal life. We will return to Asa later in the book and break down how she was able to succeed at the Name Game using her creativity tools and processes. While the Name Game does not have a business outcome, we will move creativity into the workplace where it can spark innovation, communication, problem resolution, and fun.

We applaud lifelong learners who are always searching for new ideas, new sparks, and new ways to solve problems. Creativity, both the tools and approaches offered within this book, can be a spark in your lifelong journey of *becoming more.*

PART 1
The Case for Creativity

CHAPTER 1

What Creativity Means

Creativity is the unique and defining trait of our species; and its ultimate goal, self-understanding. —EDWARD WILSON

In the late 1990s, NASA launched a mission to Mars named the Martian Climate Orbiter. Its primary objective was to determine the distribution of water on Mars and monitor weather conditions. During the mission, the Orbiter was to communicate with a lander on Mars's surface, sending data back to NASA for analysis. Unfortunately, there was a communications problem. It appears there was a misunderstanding of terms and measurement systems being used for the path of the Orbiter. NASA provided the data program (which used the United States Customary Unit), while the part responsible for completing the calculations was provided by a critical contractor, who used the NASA Standard Software Interface Specification. Apples talking to oranges. In the exact science of NASA, where inches matter, the Orbiter path's calculation was off, causing the Orbiter to miss its trajectory and ultimately ricochet into the uppermost atmosphere where it was lost. Working with a common agreement or definition is vital to NASA missions, but also in our work lives. Do we have a common agreement on what the term *creativity* means?

Organization work is often muddled by terms that have multiple meanings. A combination of academics, authors, and practitioners redefine the same terms causing multiple meanings. Often, we do not check to see that we are on the same page. Examples of ambiguous terms include *innovation, talent, teams,* and *leadership.* It is worth it to spend the time to define terms so that we don't ricochet into the wrong atmosphere.

Invaded Terms: Guilty as Charged

Consider the invaded term *creativity.* An *invaded term* is a common term that's been taken hostage by someone who plunders its original meaning to fit their purposes. The more this happens, the more the term loses a shared meaning. The term was first used in 1875 by Adolphus William Ward to describe Shakespeare's poetic "creativity," although it did not see common usage until WWII. As an invaded term, *creativity* has acquired different shades of meanings that include original ideas, novelty, artistic work production, the creation of ideas, effective, useful, utility, imagination, innovation, and invention. One of our favorite definitions belongs to Robert E. Franken, who says creativity is a "tendency to generate or recognize ideas, alternatives, or possibilities that may be useful in solving problems, communicating with others, and entertaining ourselves and others."

We are guilty of invading the term creativity to fulfill the promise of this book. Our definition draws on the key definitions that came before us, but it is unique; it adds context. For this book, we define creativity as:

> The ability to recognize or generate ideas through novel perspectives that defy the crowd and create aha moments.

Our promise for this book includes deconstructing the morass of information on creativity to provide a purposeful and practical way to bring more creativity into organizations and personal lives (Figure 1-1). Let's break down our definition:

- **Recognize.** While many believe that only creatives generate the ideas, it should be noted that leaders who can recognize creativity have an important role. Often in organizations, it is these recognizers who remove barriers for the creatives to succeed.

- **Generate.** We will look at the roots of the word creativity shortly, but for now, we like that notion of bringing something out of the dark into the world. Creativity has to come out of your head or your heart and into your environment. Otherwise, what good is it?
- **Novel perspectives.** Creativity in and of itself may not solve problems. However, it does create unique perspectives that are essential to solving many of the vexing problems we face. These perspectives can be new to the world or new to your organization.
- **Defies the crowd.** Creativity overturns orthodoxies and goes against the grain. It is frame-breaking. *Defying the crowd* is our shorthand for going against the norm. Again, we offer context in our definition—in this case, to go against the crowd where the crowd is those around us who are holders of the status quo. Additionally, we are often part of the crowd that critiques our own ideas, pushing against our creativity.
- **Aha moments.** An aha moment is a moment of sudden inspiration, insight, recognition, or comprehension. Creativity should engender an aha moment and an emotional reaction that affirms its gift to the problem at hand.

Figure 1-1. Creativity Defined

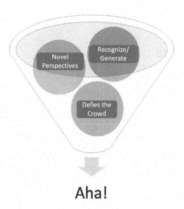

Aha!

Creativity Forward

Building on this definition, we looked at the origin of the word. Creativity's etymological roots are from the Latin verb *creare*, meaning to bring something forth. We like the movement associated with creare—bringing something out of the dark into the world. It's not enough to think creatively, you must do something with it. Unleash it into the world, bring it forth. We like this notion of movement in creativity. We refer to it as *creativity forward*, bringing your creativity out of your head and heart and into the world, and paying it forward to elicit creativity from others.

Creativity forward has interesting added qualities. It speaks to always pursuing creativity but never quite getting there. To keep tinkering. It connotes lifelong learning to become more creative. It speaks to the movement, not the destination. Creativity forward is both a concept and an encouragement. It's the birth of moving creativity from nature to nurture, adding panache and confidence.

Creativity forward also draws on the courage needed to fulfill part of the definition. To defy the crowd, and even oneself, in the act of creativity is not an easy thing to do. We suggest that when people think they are not creative, it is not that they don't have creative ability; it is that they may not have tapped into the courage required to unleash their creativity into the world. Creativity forward is a rallying cry to mobilize ourselves to defy the crowd.

Your Creativity Muse

The word *muse* stems from Greek and Roman mythology, describing a spirit who presides over artistic disciplines. We are using the word to refer to a person in your life who serves as one of your creative inspirations. Use the "Your Creativity Muse" exercise to think about someone in your life, professional or personal, who you believe is extremely creative. Try not to use an artist, poet, or someone already in the creative world. See the appendix for a completed example.

🎨 Journal Exercise: Your Creativity Muse

My muse:

1. How did they demonstrate creativity?
Did their creativity touch on these parts of our definition: recognize, generate, novel perspectives, defy the crowd, aha moments?

> Creativity Doodle

2. Why does this example resonate with you?

> Creativity Doodle

3. What are your takeaways either about how to demonstrate creativity or how it affects you when you see it?

> Creativity Doodle

Human vs. Machine Creativity

News about machines taking over our jobs inundates our everyday lives. Will machine learning or artificial intelligence (AI) ever replace human creativity? At this point, we can say that in most countries, to receive a patent on a new product, the inventor has to be a human. While problem solving is within the domain of machine learning (with limitations), problem finding is not, at least not now. A likely scenario now might be for humans to identify new questions or identify new problems that humans and AI solve together. For now, creativity, as we have defined it in this book, is still the unique domain of humans.

But AI can augment human creativity. Presently AI can only choose between the data inputted into it by humans, and cannot choose between imagined options. That may change in the future, but pure creativity is still a uniquely human trait. Even if machines cannot replace humans in the creative domain, they can complement human creativity. But is AI creative? We've learned where AI is concerned, never say never.

Compare and Contrast

We defined creativity as recognizing or generating ideas through novel perspectives that defy the crowd and create aha moments. We created this definition to focus on professionals in organizations, such as talent development professionals, who use creativity to solve their internal partners' or customers' problems. This brings up the question of how creativity, as defined here, relates to other practices that, on their surface, seem similar or identical to creativity? Let's compare and contrast a few:

- **Innovation.** Innovation is the process of translating an idea or invention into a good or service that creates value or for which customers will pay. While there is some overlap, innovation is clearly focused on value extraction from the end-user or customer who values the solution. With that said, creativity is an essential ingredient at critical points, particularly divergent points, through the innovation process.

- **Invention.** Invention is the act of conceiving something that has never been made or used before. Creativity is a necessary component in invention, but the two are not the same.
- **Craft.** Craft or crafting is an activity involving skill in making things by hand. If you are the originator of a craft, likely you used creativity in its creation. If you are making the craft, you are likely following instructions and may not be using your full potential creativity to do so.
- **Design.** Steve Jobs defined design as "not just what it looks like and feels like. Design is how it works." Design is a user-centered plan and specification for the construction of an object, system, or process. It indeed uses creativity throughout the process, but it is not the same as creativity.
- **Imagination.** The act or power of forming a mental image of something that has never existed either in the senses or in reality. Imagination is an ingredient of creativity, and vice versa, but they have vastly different roles in bringing creativity out into the light.
- **Fantasy.** The power or process of creating unrealistic or improbable mental images, such as a daydream. Again, creativity is at play, but our creativity has to lead to something realistic and probable.

An Example of Creativity in the Workplace

We started this chapter with an example from NASA about definitions. So it is perhaps fitting that NASA provides an unexpected example of creativity in the workplace from our own lives. When we worked for Whirlpool Corporation, one of our annual assignments in the TD area was to design the annual leadership conference for the senior leadership group. We based our design on current issues the CEO and executive committee wanted to explore. That year, they wanted to explore how hard it is to speak up when you see something that is not right. To bring the workshop to life, we decided to take the leadership group to NASA's Kennedy Space Center at Cape Canaveral, Florida, to learn firsthand about the *Challenger* disaster.

The Space Shuttle *Challenger* disaster on January 28, 1986, centered around O-rings and their failure at cold temperatures. The O-ring was known to be sensitive to cold below 53 degrees. The weather on the day of launch was 36 degrees. Why would NASA go ahead with the launch knowing that the O-rings could fail? There are many case studies of why NASA launched *Challenger* that morning. The root cause analysis centers on a host of reasons that led to the ill-fated launch; engineering, public relations, and politics are just a few or the reasons cited. We were interested in exploring the leadership failure to create an environment where people not only felt free to speak up and defy the crowd but felt accountable for doing so.

We dedicated one morning of the three-day workshop to a visit to the Kennedy Space Center. We were fortunate that we had contacts within NASA to provide our workshop participants with a behind-the-scenes experience. We lined up NASA speakers who brought the *Challenger* disaster to life in terms of leadership lessons. Many had been in leadership roles at the time of the disaster, so they had firsthand stories and lessons to share. It was very emotional to hear them speak and feel their regret for their failure to defy the crowd or create an environment where others could defy the crowd by opposing the tidal wave of PR and political forces. It was an incredible experience with brave leaders who told their story and how they changed, many saying never again would they fail to go against the crowd when they knew the crowd was wrong. The impact of their decision—lives lost—was more significant than anything most of us would face in our working lives. The experience left an indelible impression.

In the afternoon we returned to our hotel conference room and had a short debrief on the NASA experience. Our plan did not consider how emotional the visit would be for our leaders or how, during their ride back, they would reflect on their failures, personal and professional, to defy the crowd, in both big and small ways.

Once we finished the debrief, we got ready to move to the next business topic. Suddenly, however, someone interrupted and said, "I don't know about anyone else, but I'm not ready to move on. I want to talk about this more." Then, to everyone's surprise, he walked to the front of the conference room and started sharing how deeply the visit had affected him, reflecting on his failures to take a stand in large and small situations. He vowed on that day to work on defying the crowd when he thought it was headed in the wrong direction. Others followed, walking to the front of the room and sharing their emotional reaction to the morning and their leadership lessons learned around creating an environment where people feel safe to speak up when they see something concerning. As the workshop facilitators, we watched this unfold and called an audible (that is, we changed course)—we scrapped the entire afternoon's agenda. We then did something we'd never done before; we turned the meeting over to the participants. It was an afternoon that none of us would forget.

Let's use our creativity definition as a lens to assess what happened as we, the workshop designers, used creativity to pitch the idea of taking the workshop to NASA. The day we went in to pitch the NASA visit idea to the CEO is sealed in our memory. We had never done anything like this; it was big and bold and risky. We had no idea how the CEO would react. He immediately felt the aha moment of the idea and jumped in to co-create critical aspects of the experience. He thought it was unique, offering a novel perspective, an aha moment; it defied the norm.

However, there is another crucial creativity lesson in the story, one that had nothing to do with our actions. When the workshop participants stood up and took control of the meeting by sharing personal stories of how the visit affected them, group creativity took over. They had their own perspective on how best to spend the rest of the day; they shared their moments of struggle to defy norms in their professional lives. And while none of their experiences had resulted in anything near the *Challenger* scale, they certainly felt the weight of going along with the crowd when they thought the crowd was not right. By taking over the workshop to do what they collectively felt in the moment, they turned around our notion of who runs a leadership development workshop, or who *should* run it. Our only creative contribution at that point was to recognize it and get out of the way. At that point, we became recognizers of creativity.

What Am I Hiring Creativity to Do?

In the innovation world, Clayton Christensen was a giant. One of the tools he gave us was to think about a product or service in terms of what you are "hiring" it to do. He called the tool "Jobs to Be Done." We want you to use this same logic in terms of creativity. In the next chapter, we will explore why creativity matters. It will be a more wide-reaching discussion on creativity in terms of individuals, teams, and organizations. To help you prepare for that chapter, let's explore what you are hiring creativity to do for you in your professional or personal life. Figure 1-2 presents some options to start your thinking. They come from the creative workshops we have conducted over the years.

Figure 1-2. What Am I Hiring Creativity to Do?

• Self-actualize—to realize my true potential.	• Instill courage.
• Problem solve for my job.	• Explore possibilities.
• Think in new ways.	• Break up boredom in my daily life; provide a diversion.
• Do things in new ways.	• Purge demons.
• Enhance my storytelling skills.	• Have fun.
• Give me some personal panache.	• Create curiosity.
• Jump-start a new career.	• Complete my job.

In addition to myths and enemies, we will encourage you to reflect on what you have hired creativity to do in the "Jobs to Be Done" exercise. Think of three areas of your life where creativity could produce new outcomes. What are different jobs for creativity? What could you hire creativity to do? Be as varied as you can. Please also draw your concept, no matter how rudimentary. No one is really looking. Go ahead, defy the crowd with your drawings! What three things will you hire creativity to do?

🎨 Journal Exercise: Jobs to Be Done

What three things will you hire creativity to do? In the spaces below, write out and sketch your concepts.

Example 1

Creativity Doodle

Example 2

Creativity Doodle

Example 3

Creativity Doodle

The One Thing: Defy the Crowd

There is a great deal to think about in terms of the meaning of creativity. It's an invaded term thrown around a great deal without a shared understanding. We believe our definition—*recognize or generate ideas through novel perspectives that defy the crowd and create aha moments*—offers a concise and comprehensive way to define creativity within organizations.

The part of the definition that we want to emphasize is defying a crowd, where the crowd includes yourself. We are often our own worst enemy to our creativity. In fact, at the top of the enemies list, most of us should write "me." The one thing that we want you to begin to experiment with is defying the crowd.

Perhaps, just for fun, think about Asa and Tim in the Name Game from the introduction. Asa defies the crowd at every turn, even though she did not have an audience. Tim feels pressure from the crowd, even though there is no one watching. His own mind stopped him from misnaming objects in the room.

We would like you to try the exercise again with a mindful intention of defying the crowd. Go into it with the idea that you will delight in misnaming things. Get more comfortable with the creativity of it. Take note of how you react to something you are about to say or do that is creative. And then, as Asa did, throw caution to the wind and try it. We promise you will not cause clocks to stop or a tsunami to engulf the earth. It will be OK. Put your best creativity foot forward and defy the crowd, starting with yourself.

In the next chapter, we will look at individual creativity and why it matters as a purpose-finding and sense-making endeavor and that humans need to survive and thrive. Before you read chapter 2, take a pause and imagine your world without creativity, either creativity that you generate or creativity that you appreciate in your day-to-day life. If what appears to you with in this moment is a black void, keep reading to understand why filling that space with creativity is so important in our lives.

CHAPTER 2

Why Creativity Matters

Let's start by asking, "Should we really have to call this out? Do we have to address why creativity matters?"

The answer is yes! We humans get stuck. We get stuck with seeing or doing things the way we've always done them because that's how we are naturally wired. We are predisposed to look for patterns consciously and subconsciously. It is how we survive. Pattern recognition is an automatic organizing system for our brains—to recognize objects and situations, look for patterns—so we can quickly focus on doing other things, such as learning a new language, developing a unique skill set, or solving a complex problem.

"Free Your Mind, and the Rest Will Follow" —En Vogue

Here's an "insider scoop." There is a connection between pattern recognition and creativity. We all have the innate ability to create and be creative, and it doesn't start with discovering untapped courage. The key is to recognize patterns and then allow yourself to be curious enough to find the connections between what may seemingly be disparate things, topics, or experiences. It's that simple. Be curious.

In the spirit of keeping things simple, let's take a look at Carl the Caveman. It's an ordinary day for Carl; he has found a patch of root vegetables springing up between some rocks in the ground, so he's clearing the rocks to get to his food source. Carl begins removing rocks and throws each one into a pile with the same movement and force he does any time he works with rocks. When he throws rocks onto a pile he hears a thud. Today, Carl notices that something happens. He throws a rock on the pile and sees a small flash of light while he hears the thud. He notices a kind of fog and smells something he's never smelled before. At that very moment, Carl has a choice—continue throwing rocks, listen to the thud, and go about his day as normal, or to stop and be curious about what happens when two specific rocks hit each other. So, let's assume that Carl chose to be curious, and we'll give him credit for discovering fire. Now, seriously think about this: If Carl had not chosen to explore what he experienced during his usual routine, to question the pattern that he had become accustomed to, we could all still be living in a Paleolithic Era.

"Imagine" — John Lennon

Living, working, and surviving in today's volatile, uncertain, complex, and ambiguous (VUCA) environment means the need to create is not only for those who are considered top talent, nor can it be a one-time event. The integration of creative habits into our everyday thinking and way of being is critical. It is non-negotiable. The good news is that creativity is a natural and renewable resource. It is also a resource that requires nurturing, and if it's not purposefully cultivated, it will become stagnant.

Imagine the possibilities for organizations where people are viewed and respected as naturally creative regardless of role or level in the organization. Organizations would be overflowing with people who feel valued, fulfilled, and engaged. People would be embracing diversity of thought and the inclusion of ideas, working together as high performing teams; exploring ideas; and achieving and exceeding expectations of themselves *and* the organization. While these phrases have become buzz terms and, to some, just words on a wall sign or website, it is what we want for our organizations, isn't it? And, if we're honest, it's the kind of environment we all want to be part of: An environment that believes in and fosters true belonging. And with belonging comes freedom. Freedom to be who we are called to be. Freedom to not be concerned about the repercussions of authentically showing up. Freedom to be curious and uncover novel perspectives, generate new ideas, defy the crowd and the status quo, and create experiences, products, and services that evoke an aha moment!

So, what does true belonging look like, if even for a moment? Let's go back to July 15, 1985. The time, 7 p.m. The location, the UK's Wembley Stadium. The event, Live Aid. The band, Queen. A highlight of that performance was Freddie Mercury leading a crowd of 72,000 people in a vocal riff of "Day O." Arms raised in the air, voices singing in unison, echoing throughout the stadium and the world. No one was concerned about being on or off-key; no one knew where he was going with the song or what was coming next. It didn't matter—Freddie was creating in the moment, and the crowd of 72,000 people came alongside to co-create with him. They were so in the flow of the moment and what was being brought forth that they had no idea that the experience being created would become a historical milestone examined and re-examined by sociologists, psychologists, and music historians. This event now serves as a muse to show how creativity can bring forth a sense of belonging. Belonging stretched its arms outside Wembley Stadium to welcome 1.9 billion people across 150 countries to come alongside and engage in the shared experience.

"I've Got the Music in Me" —The Kiki Dee Band

Music was the avenue used by this leader to create a safe space for people to express openly, create collectively, and bring forth their voices in a harmonious sound that made a lasting impact in history. Music is a creative outlet that unifies through a magnetic force where each person has their individual experience. Yet, there can also be a collective sense of belonging. In some instances, such as Queen and Live Aid, there appeared a euphoric sense of belonging.

Close your eyes and remember scenes of evening balcony concerts in Italy during the summer of 2020. People walking along the street stopped. They paused their busyness to experience the moment, to be in the moment to witness the creative spirit of a person who, yes, may have been incredibly talented with a specific instrument. Still, even more significant than that, the musician recognized a need to create an experience where people could be "free." Free, if at least for a moment, from the pressures of living amid a global pandemic.

Music has an unexplainable and inescapable presence; it is accessible and approachable to all. Marvin Gaye and Tammi Terrell's "Ain't No Mountain High Enough" can raise people's spirits and be a source of strength and beacon of brighter days ahead. Samuel Barber's "Adagio for Strings," which premiered in 1938, is a short, powerful work—one of empathy and compassion. It has a personality that can "be with" people during their lowest of lows, bringing forth emotions at the very core of what it means to be human. Music is a conduit of time travel. Within 11 seconds of hearing the piano roll, we are on our feet, ready to move and groove to ABBA's "Dancing Queen," creating our own dances, youthful, unapologetically unabandoned, and in the moment. We are simultaneously in two places, the mind in the past, body in the present.

Music is one example of creativity, and so many people think it is only accessible to a few; however, this isn't the case. The lyrics and hip hop beat of the Sean Forbes song "I'm Deaf" are an educational bridge to those in the hearing world who think that people who are deaf cannot experience music. Sean's song and view on life provide creative inspiration to others who are deaf or hard of hearing and seek to express themselves, to defy the crowd who says that something isn't possible because they don't hear the way others hear. In my personal experience, I've found that those who are deaf hear better than those who have what is considered "normal hearing" because of their ability to sense and feel throughout their bodies and their ability to truly listen.

Music is accessible to everyone. Some of us hear the melody and tap our feet; others feel the beat in their chest and in their very core. Some choose to create an interpretive dance, while others choose to sit and soak in the experience. Individual and collective reactions to music are forms of creativity because of something being called forth from inside the self. But many of us don't realize that we're creative! We're creating! We prefer to give the credit to someone else, if at all.

"Fearfully and Wonderfully Made" —Psalm 139:14

So, is the question "why does creativity matter?" or is it "where can people tap into and live in their natural creative ability?" It is about shifting your mindset. What if creativity can be discovered, taught, and nurtured? What if regular and repeated use of a simple process and simple tools would allow people to look at the world in new ways? What if it's about tapping into solving problems with child-like curiosity? What if creativity is about opening up space—a mental and emotional space where people own and appreciate how they are creative and how their creativity contributes to the greater good, whether it's an organizational strategy, daily operations, or approaching problems in everyday life. What if solving problems, creating new solutions, and innovation are about how to view patterns differently?

Steve Jobs once said, "Creativity is just connecting things. When you ask creative people how they did something, they feel a little guilty because they didn't really do it; they just saw something. It seemed obvious to them after a while." What's great about this statement is the last three words, "after a while." While creativity is a natural resource to all of us, it can get buried, and so it may take a while to resurface and come back to life. It's also important to realize that each of us is creative in our own way—there's no one way to be creative.

Creativity is about the diverging and converging of ideas. Tight deadlines, the pressure to excel, and providing financial results take precedence over allowing time and space for people to explore thoughts and ideas, search for inspiration, and smash together unrelated ideas or things to gain a new perspective. The problem with having no time or space is that the status quo will remain, and yet, shareholders are seeking novel views and new ideas. Many organizations have a mindset that only a few can create because they are trained to. These people typically sit in an innovation lab, graphic design role, or marketing function, and they are essentially developed and paid to be creative. At the same time, people across the organization are expected to creatively solve problems. However, since they're not paid to be creative, they aren't trained on how to bring forth their creativity to solve problems. It's an interesting pattern of thinking, orthodoxy, and dynamic. We expect creativity from everyone, but don't have time for everyone to be creative because there's a business to run. So, what if every person in your organization was seen as naturally creative?

"Shining Star" — Earth, Wind & Fire

As talent development professionals, we have a unique opportunity. First, we see employees as humans (at least we hope you do, otherwise we need to have a completely different conversation). It is our responsibility to foster an ecosystem where unique creative abilities are recognized and celebrated. Fostering the ecosystem starts with a choice, and we're presenting this choice to you right now. You have a choice about how you will show up and be a role model for enabling people to authentically create.

A starting place for being a role model is to choose to see how creative superpowers show up in everyday interactions with other people. Here's a scenario to get you started: You've been tapped to lead a project to build and implement a new performance management framework within the next two months. Mateo, Robin, Kris, and Paola are your assigned cross-functional and global project team members. You think to yourself, "Wow! Two months to get this project up and off the ground. That's a short timeframe, but we can make this happen. We've gotta leverage each other's strengths and stick to a solid project plan." You call together a project kick-off meeting to get after this body of work, and it's during the get-to-know-you phase of the meeting you uncover the following insights about your team:

- Mateo is part of the research and development function and an engineer by trade. He asks *a lot* of questions; it's evident that a thorough understanding of the project scope and expectations is essential to him as he mentally processes how he can support the project. His experience with root cause analysis, ability to interpret data, and influence with decision makers is recognized throughout the organization.

- Robin has recent experience with investment in two online start-up companies. She is a self-proclaimed serial entrepreneur who *loves* to brainstorm and think about big wild ideas. She's excited about the opportunity to blow up the current performance management program and support change management efforts in her global communications function.

- Kris works within HR to administer the talent management system. She has a side hustle as a professional organizer, where she gets a lot of energy in figuring out how things fit together most efficiently and effectively. She warned the team that she has been known to organize her friend's refrigerators without being asked.

- Paola considers herself a fixer. While her roots are in human resources, she decided to leave HR to work in various business functions for the past eight years. She thought HR moved too slowly and has now found great satisfaction by working in the business to identify problems, develop solutions, and move to speedy implementation. She takes pride in her ability to quickly produce results.

On the one hand, you have a dream team; these individuals bring diverse knowledge, skills, experiences, and perspectives. On the other hand, your team will need direction, guidance, and love from you. You've gained insights into where they get their energy and what makes their eyes shine. You're starting to look at the phases of the project you know need to happen and thinking through where each person will be in their sweet spot, happy place, creative flow, or whatever you want to call it. Your gut is also telling you that it may be a challenge to collectively get the team to move efficiently through the project process. Each person will find specific parts of the project more engaging than others due to their creative flow, team dynamics, and, ultimately, project scope, budget, and deadline.

Now is when you ask yourself, "What if?" What if we created a project team charter, so each person has the opportunity to articulate how they want to show up for this project? What if we were a project team that kicked butt in a way that no other project team has before? What if we fail? What if we challenged ourselves to recognize patterns of thinking that could hold us back? What if we created a performance management program where people are recognized across the board for their unique talents?

"Ain't No Stoppin' Us Now" —McFadden & Whitehead

Just by asking "what if," you've started to build one of your creative thinking muscles by consciously breaking out of your usual pattern of thinking, and the coolest thing is that you didn't have to sign up for a gym membership. As you may have heard, developing new habits requires purposeful integration into everyday activities or workflows. The key is to set aside time, make space, create rituals to cultivate, and repeatedly practice or use the new skill.

Creative problem solving is rooted in pattern recognition—similar to a doctor diagnosing an ailment. The doctor looks at the symptoms and puts them together to see what makes sense by combining what they've been taught in medical school and professional externships. The doctor recognizes patterns, connects the dots, and makes a diagnosis and recommended treatment.

The same applies to how we view challenges or problems. We go through the same process as the doctor by relying on our knowledge, skills, and experiences to diagnose and solve a problem. The challenge is that many of us are not trained doctors, nor are we being asked to diagnose and fix a physiological ailment. However, we are expected to solve some complex issues that can be described as the size of a 600-pound octopus measuring 30 feet across with tentacles eight feet long!

We recognize and honor that the audience reading this book is comprised of individuals from different industries, stages of life, work experiences, and global perspectives. To meet you where you are now or wherever you are striving to go, we are choosing to keep our views relevant, practical, and inspirational. We encourage you to stay with us, trust the process, allow yourself to step out of your comfort zone, be open and vulnerable (which is also part of the creative process), and be curious enough to see what happens.

Now, take a minute to work through the "What If?" exercise on the next two pages. You can take what you learn and immediately use within your organization.

The One Thing: Human Beings Not Performance Beings

Notice the use of "people" and "humans" throughout this chapter rather than the label "employee." If you take anything away from reading this book, remember that pure creativity is a natural human trait. Only humans can gather and pool knowledge to gain insights, ideate on those insights, and create. It just so happens that humans can also be employees; the key is never to forget that employees are people—humans with the ability to create, positively impact the bottom line, and, most importantly, make a difference in our world.

You're all primed with how you can change the world—your world and that of others—just by inserting "what if" into your way of thinking and the conversations that you're having. Moving into chapter 3 we will continue to wear our honesty badges and will be looking at barriers to creativity, and tactics you can take to recognize and deal with the barriers.

🎨 Journal Exercise: What If?

1. Write a short paragraph about a current situation you view as a challenge or problem.

2. Now, reframe the challenge or problem as an opportunity by writing one "what if" statement.

3. Write three additional "what if" statements about the same opportunity.

1.

2.

3.

⊘ Journal Exercise: What If? (cont.)

4. What's it like for you to see the previous challenge or problem as an opportunity?

5. How will you incorporate "what if" into your thought processes and conversations within the next 24 hours?

CHAPTER 3

Barriers to Creativity

In the movie *Adaptation*, actor Nicholas Cage as the protagonist and screenwriter Charlie Kaufman is staring at a blank sheet of paper in his typewriter carriage. There is a look of equal parts panic and loathing in his eyes. He is trying to find his writing muse to fulfill a looming script deadline. Writers, who know all too well what he is going through, no longer refer to this as writer's block but as the banana-nut-muffin-problem—it's their version of creativity torture. A voiceover of his inner dialogue tells us what he is thinking:

> To begin. . . . To begin. . . . How to start? I'm hungry. I should get coffee. Coffee would help me think. Maybe I should write something first, then reward myself with coffee. Coffee and a muffin. OK, so I need to establish the themes. Maybe a banana-nut. That's a good muffin.

In this chapter, we will discuss obstacles to doing something creative. We will discuss barriers in three subgroups: teams, organizations, and individuals. First, let's look at some overarching myths of creativity that abound in many organizations.

Creativity Myths

In the introduction to this book, we presented Asa and Tim as they went through the Name Game creativity exercise. Asa excelled while Tim struggled. Many of us believe we are more like Tim than Asa. While we don't know their background or their Mensa scores, we know that Asa was not born a creativity genius and that Tim did not come out of the womb a creativity oaf. Tim has other strengths. He is an analytical savant but struggles with creativity. Asa trained herself to be more creative. Mindfully, she has learned to defy the expectations about how it should be, or what the right answer is, and has leaned into creative absurdity. Asa was not thinking about being judged, getting the correct answer, or delivering value. She learned to free herself from these yokes and put herself in the moment. She knows that there is a time to create and a time to judge in most creative work in companies.

By participating in an exercise such as the Name Game we can reflect on what might be holding us back from being more creative. Myths of creativity blocking our progress might include:

- Creativity comes from nature. Nature implies you are born with it; nurture implies you can learn it.
- You have to be in the arts to be creative.
- Creativity is not practical.
- Companies don't want works of art; they want products and services that work.
- Creativity and boundaries are antithetical.
- Creativity is a puff of white smoke, unexplainable and mysterious. No one knows where it comes from; therefore, it is not repeatable.
- Companies don't want us to be creative; they want us to stay in our box.
- You can hire professionals to fulfill all your organization's creativity requirements.
- You lose creativity over time. Once we become adults, creativity is erased.
- Creativity is only practiced if you are not under a time crunch.

As Asa learned before we met her in the Name Game exercise, we, along with Tim, will learn how to improve our creative skills and self-identify as a creative. Creativity is available to each of us; we can learn and nurture it over time.

Team Barriers: Permission to Be Creative

We often run open enrollment innovation workshops for participants from many diverse companies. We start by putting teams together based on their creative strengths to ensure diverse and influential teams. At the beginning of their innovation work, we find that many team members are reserved and not ready to jump in with creative ideas. This is not because they are not skilled or motivated; it is likely because they have never been asked to be creative at work. Throwing out a creative idea in a team of colleagues does take a bit of getting used to. To counter this, we work hard to make safe spaces with ground rules that include creating without judgment. We role model the creative behaviors we are hoping for so participants can see that nothing bad happens when we throw out a creative idea.

In addition, we often add an extra step during the first creative exercise where the participants are ideating, which we call "permission to innovate." For example, say we are ideating on orthodoxies related to a coffee experience. We facilitate the participants through the first ideation round to assess how comfortable they are with tossing out creative ideas. If they are holding back, as most new teams do, we say, "Now in this next round we want the most ridiculous, nonsensical idea that you have. In fact, there is a fun prize for the most unsuspected idea." This is often enough to get participants to overcome their creativity jitters. It's a comment on our organizations that we need permission to be creative. We have all learned through trial and error to stay in our lane and not be too creative, lest we are judged as not practical.

Defying team pressure to be creative is something we deal with all of our lives. As children, defying the crowd to be creative may result in being bullied or ostracized. As working adults, the fear of not fitting in or being laughed at is so ingrained that many of us choose to go along with the crowd, even when we believe the crowd could use some creativity to advance their work. We shut down and put our creativity on sleep mode to avoid judgment. Stepping out from the team is not about being rude or under-participating in the team's activities. It takes some individual will to start applying creativity in a team that is otherwise not creative. In this section, we will look at what it takes to be a creative team member. In chapter 9, we will discuss what it takes to be a creative team leader or facilitator.

Most teams don't live in a creative space; they are too busy trying to get the job done and are often time-starved. Even teams that are chartered with creativity, such as innovation teams, need to be creative and attentive to avoid falling into the ease of the status quo. There are so many daily pressures in organization life that it seems easier to just deliver the mail than to find new ways or spaces. Here are some ideas about how to help the team bring in more creativity:

- **Meet with the team leader or sponsor.** If you are a team member, even if you have been on the team for some time, plan a discussion with the team leader. Acquaint yourself with what they are trying to do—politely prod for creativity tolerance. Discuss areas where you would like to help infuse more creativity.

- **Be clear on the team charter and strategy linkage.** Take time to revisit the team charter. If one does not exist, create what you think the charter is from the meeting outcomes or ask the leader. Also, take time to understand how your team relates to the business strategy. This will help you know how hard to push in getting to a more creative outcome.

- **Experiment.** Introduce creative experimentation to help the team achieve its goals. One of the best tools to introduce creativity, especially in a creativity-unfriendly (or uninitiated) environment, is to ask for permission to experiment. Your experiment might involve using a creativity tool, freeing up thinking with a creativity exercise, and looking in unrelated areas to find nuggets that help the team uncover opportunities using creativity. If you ask for permission to run a rapid experiment, your team will know that what is about to happen won't count if it does not work, and thus will buy in more readily. There is almost no downside. Once you introduce a little bit of creativity, more will follow; it's like priming the pump.

- **Model the behavior.** Another way to infuse creativity into your team is to model it for others. When there is a question or an exercise, use your creativity skills to introduce new opportunities. If someone tries something creative, support their endeavor and give them positive feedback.

- **Enlist other creatives.** Look around on your team and find other creatives to form a bond with them. You can rely on each other or work as a sub-team to infuse creativity into the team.

Teams offer an excellent venue for creativity. While this is especially true if the leader creates the right environment, it is not just about the leader; team members can also bring their own creative skills to benefit the team. As a team member, there is much you can do. As you join future teams, we offer you a challenge. We would like you to go to a fresh page in your creativity journal and write the following statement in gigantic uppercase letters:

THE TEAM IS MORE CREATIVE BECAUSE I'M A MEMBER!

If you take this challenge to heart, you will feel a commitment to help your teams use creativity to solve the organization's problems. You don't need to be the leader or sponsor to raise the creative index of the team. Chapter 6 will help you create or hone your creative process. With repetition and practice, your creativity confidence will soar, and you will have various approaches for assisting every team you encounter.

We've shared a starter list of some actions you can take to increase team creativity as a team member. Now use the "My Most Creative Team Experience" exercise on the next page to think about a time you worked creatively in a team.

🎨 Journal Exercise: My Most Creative Team Experience

1. Think back over the teams you have been on, in any capacity (work, volunteer, personal). Select the one experience you think was most creative.

2. Describe and sketch what you and others did to make it so creative.
Did you break the norms and go to new spaces? Did you apply a new idea or technology? Did the team have a deep creative experience that bonded the group? Was there a creative sage in the group that helped everyone be more creative?

3. Describe and sketch the feelings of being in that group.
Think back on how you felt at the most creative time for the team. Note your inner thoughts and feelings.

Now let's look at creativity through an organizational lens, with both intended and unintended consequences.

Organizational Barriers: Please Leave Your Creativity at Home

We were both fortunate to work for many great companies where we traveled the world, working on creative and innovative projects. In those travels, we met many amazing people and had wonderful experiences of bringing new products and services to the world. When we reflect on the most significant lessons from our creative endeavors, the notion of underground creativity rises to the top—that there is an untapped reserve of creativity that organizations often fail to unleash.

We soon realized that many people in these companies could not bring their creative side to work. As Nancy's colleague Professor Harry Davis observes:

> Many people drive to work and feel that they have to put parts
> of themselves in their car's trunk. They leave their whole person
> behind and try to fit into what they think is the company mold.

The Creatives

We find this is especially true with creativity. We work with so many people who have fantastic creative pursuits outside the office, yet they aren't comfortable bringing their creative side to work.

At Whirlpool, we decided to lean into the problem of leaving your whole person in the car. We started an affinity group called the Creatives, a network of more than 100 people who self-organized to become more creative. We began by hosting meet-and-greet functions where the only agenda item was to get to know other creatives. We called these social events Pints and Pencils. One of the founding members, Chris Gregory, described his first exposure to the Whirlpool Creatives this way: The groups of creatives "didn't necessarily work together, but it forced you to sit at a table and realize there's a cross-pollination of skill sets. I didn't know at first all of what it entailed, but [I] joined anyway. I don't think I've seen this at any organization I've been at before." It was a big reason why he stayed attracted to Whirlpool. The Creatives provided an outlet for people to bring their creative spirit to work and not leave it in their car's trunk.

Over time the Creatives became known as a hotspot for creativity. When innovation teams needed to infuse new thinking into their ideas, they invited members from the Creatives to join. When a new headquarters was being designed, the facilities group asked subgroups of the Creatives to help them design sections of the building. The Creatives set up a website to host their work, and it was awe-inspiring. Midcentury furniture design, jazz ensembles, sculpture, crafts, stand-up comedy, and performance art were just a few of the talents featured. The Creatives did something else unique; they invited others in the company and the local community to join the group, helping these new members unleash their hidden creative talents. The Creatives also took their creativity out into the community, assisting nonprofits in bringing more creativity into their offerings.

By itself, the Creatives did not solve the problem of allowing people to bring their whole selves to work, but we think it made a dent in unleashing creativity within the organization. It stands as an excellent example of how companies can encourage creativity from everyone.

How Companies Put Up Barriers

Most organizations were not built from day one to be creative. They were built to celebrate zero variation, predictability, and sticking to one's knitting. There are visible and hidden barriers to creativity in most organizations. It does not take much pushback for people to realize that they had better leave their creative self in the trunk of their car. Many organizational cultures reward sameness and punish creativity. After the dot-com bust of the late 1990s and the early 2000s, companies became skeptical of creativity; the word even became taboo. In one company we worked with, if you were seen as creative, you were labeled as too "touchy-feely," which did not bode well in your performance reviews. In a direct and heavy-handed way, this company bullied creativity.

Talent pool managers often have a list of competencies that are the scorecard that gets one promoted. Look within your organization at the talent pool descriptors; we doubt that you will find "creative" on the list. The term, by itself, is not how you get your ticket punched. On the contrary, to be called creative in a company can often be code for not getting things done.

Creativity as the Sidekick

Creativity is usually not the lead in the movie; it is usually the friend next door whose fundamental role is to help the protagonist realize their true potential. In other words, creativity is a sidekick in many organizations. According to Gary Susman's 2013 *Rolling Stone* article "The 21 Greatest Sidekicks in Movie History":

> Being a sidekick used to be a lot simpler in the old days. Sure, you had to let the main character play quarterback, but you still got to be the ironic truth-teller . . . you still got credit for loyalty and bravery, as long as you had the protagonist's back when it counted. Those were the basic rules of sidekicking as laid down by the father of all modern sidekicks, Sancho Panza.

For most organizations, creativity is a key performance indicator (KPI). Exceptions might include organizations whose offerings are artistic, entertainment, or curated food experiences. But for most organizations, creativity is an enabler, an expander paired with other value-creating functions such as design, innovation, or marketing. How might we migrate creativity out of the usual places and embed it as a sidekick in every part of the organization? How can talent leaders, for example, make creativity their sidekick to create more differentiated and value-creating outcomes for their organization?

Overcoming Organizational Barriers

There are many actions you can take to help your company welcome creativity. The steps you take will depend on the unique strategy, culture, and systems of your company. Here is a list of generic starter ideas for you to try or to pivot from to meet your organization's creativity needs.

- Learn how to support others to be more creative.
- Curate and move toward creative, safe spaces (more in chapters 7 and 8).
- Become a recognizer of creativity.
- Attract creatives; fashion a container in which they can percolate.
- Model creativity.
- Incentivize and reward creativity.
- Build creativity into every project, plan, workshop, or action.
- Create creativity sandboxes, with the invitation "within these boundaries, we require your creativity."
- Understand the creativity barriers in your organization and join with others to eradicate them.
- Find a set of creativity tools that can be your go-to toolkit and use them throughout the organization.
- Reduce the stigma that creativity is touchy-feely and the professional kiss of death.
- Position creativity as a sidekick in all your innovation and development processes.

The most important thing is to learn to identify which barriers of creativity are organizational versus team or individual. Sometimes we believe that if creativity is stifled, that it is a personal shortcoming. We think our team leader is not trying hard enough when often it is organizational barriers that are choking us. If you can take a balcony-view of creativity, you might find common barriers to work on or help others unleash their creativity within your organization. Use the creativity exercise on the next page to identify these organizational barriers to creativity.

🎨 Journal Exercise: Unleashing Creativity in My Organization

1. Brainstorm the top three creativity barriers in your organization.

Creativity Doodle

2. Pick one that attracts you. If you collide it with creativity, what intersections arise?

For example, if not enough time is the barrier, the creative insight might be how can I make more time? One intersection that emerges is that everyone has discretionary time at work. Think about how to attract those who want to use their discretionary time on creativity.

Creativity Doodle

3. How might you bring these solutions forward to help unleash more creativity in your organization?

You might start a Pints and Pencils affinity group or monthly creativity events in your department. Your solution will depend on your organization's traits and how much you are personally willing to invest in it.

Creativity Doodle

Every organization has barriers to creativity. If we wait for someone else to address them, they may never get fixed. Additionally, we often try to be creative in organizations, and if we fail, we think it is because we are not creative enough. Learn to recognize and differentiate between creativity barriers springing from the organization and ones that originate within you. If you see a role you can play, help your organization raise its creative index. Your effort does not have to change the enterprise; you can start within your department by using actions, both large and small, that can move the creativity needle.

Individuals: Our Barriers, Ourselves

For the first year that Nancy worked for Jeff, each time he conducted her quarterly performance review, she was sure his last line would be, "And so, we are going to have to let you go." Thankfully, that never happened.

As time went on, Nancy counted herself very lucky to work with someone of Jeff's character and caliber. As they became more comfortable with each other, they developed a repartee that worked for both. Jeff would give Nancy an out-of-the-box, complex, enterprise-wide assignment. She would ruminate on it and come back with a big, creative, new-to-the-world idea. He loved her creative panache, but her ideas were often not well-rounded from an operational perspective. Being a kind person, Jeff never shut her down. He recognized and appreciated that Nancy was uniquely qualified to go first with an untried creative idea. Jeff even joked with her by appointing her to the position of VP, No-That's-Not-It.

Instead of nixing her far-out idea, Jeff would add what he was uniquely qualified to add: his CEO financial and operational wash (no pun intended). He was able to take Nancy's idea and pivot to make it practical and workable without losing its creative zest. And it worked. Together they would create game-changing initiatives within Whirlpool.

Nancy reflects on that time and experience with Jeff this way:

> I often think that if I did not have that fun title, I would have been less willing to pitch my creative ideas to Jeff. That one fun bit permitted me to be creative. I knew he would not judge me; instead, he would take the best of my brain and the best of his brain and forge something that was both creative and practical. We worked together for 11 years that way. It is one of my most treasured and creative working relationships.

This story about Nancy's time as VP, No-That's-Not-It, offers a window into our individual barriers to creativity. Nancy realized without that shared joke she may not have been willing to bring creative ideas to Jeff.

And so we come to the last, most personal barrier. Each of us may be our own most significant barrier to creativity. Remember that famous cartoon, "We have met the enemy, and it is us"? Let's start by looking at some enemies of individual creativity, then move to strategies we can adopt to help each of us overcome the barriers we set for ourselves, knowingly or not.

The Enemies List

In addition to the myths that hold us back, there are enemies of creativity that impede our progress. While the myths we presented earlier in this chapter represent unfounded beliefs about creativity, the enemies to individual creativity are real. Here are just a few enemies to consider.

- **Exhaustion.** It's hard to be creative when you are bone-tired, and most of us are just that, tired. Often the times when we need to be creative are not when we are the most rested and alert.
- **Perfection.** Waiting until you get a perfect idea will kill creativity. For example, new writers often find that they can't write unless what comes onto the page is perfect. If they can't type

what is perfect, they often do what the protagonist in *Adaptation* did—they procrastinate and dream about banana-nut muffins. It becomes a vicious circle: See, I told you I'm not creative, just take a look at that blank page.

- **Comparison.** We spend a lot of time comparing ourselves to each other. When we do, we always come up short. You might say, "I'm not as creative as Asa," and that negative statement will cause you not even to try.

- **Self-editing.** As we form a creative idea, we tend to self-edit before allowing the idea to flourish and take shape. Sometimes we self-edit the creative idea so much that it loses its creative panache.

- **Deadlines.** We sometimes think deadlines make us less creative. They put too much pressure on us. Deadlines are a double-edged sword in terms of creativity. If you thrive on them, deadlines might add pressure for you to be creative. However, if you hate them, deadlines may add too much pressure.

- **Lack of boundaries.** Boundaries, like deadlines, have a double edge. Generally, boundaries are helpful to creativity, even though they seem like they would be detrimental. Even paintings have boundaries: the canvas.

- **Too much focus.** This one is counterintuitive as well. Sometimes when we are struggling for a creative notion or idea, we focus intently on the problem. The more we think it, the less creative it becomes. We try to force a now-or-never ultimatum on creativity.

- **Fear of the crowd.** This may be the most significant barrier to creativity. This manifests itself in two ways—fear of being judged and fear of being that lone voice. The fear of being judged is deep within us and hard to overcome. It is particularly acute in creativity; external judgment stops us from putting our ideas out there. The second part, fear of being that lone voice, is also a deeply ingrained fear. There is safety in numbers, and being a lone person opens you up to the possibility that you might be wrong and left out or left behind. It's scary to be that lone voice when you look behind you, and no one else is there.

There are countless others. But we can take this list and look for strategies to address them. In the next section we'll outline some ideas about how to coach yourself to overcome your creativity enemies.

Coaching Yourself to Higher Levels of Creativity

Creatives know the triggers that shut down their creativity, and they have learned to coach themselves into new directions. Let's take another look at the creativity enemies list we generated in the last section. However, this time we'll include examples of how to coach yourself to overcome each one.

- **Perfection.** There is an excellent saying often attributed to Voltaire: "perfect is the enemy of the good." We may want things to be so perfect that we never get creativity out from our heads or hearts into the world. One way to address this is to adopt the creativity rule: 80 percent is good enough. If you can accept this and get the idea out there, someone else will likely take it to 85 percent. That is the fantastic thing about the currency of creativity; it compounds. You never know, until you launch a creative idea out into the world, what it can become. Your creativity will compound as it gets oxygen, and it will come back to you in ways you never imagined.

- **Comparison.** One approach may be to create a creativity bubble for yourself where you can germinate ideas that do not look out and compare to others. Another way to reduce comparisons is to focus on your uniqueness. Each of us has a unique contribution to make in creativity. And it may be different from everyone else's; in fact, it should be. Your creativity is unique and therefore valuable.

- **Self-editing.** Our self-talk can wring the life out of our creative ideas. We tell ourselves how others will react, we counter our ideas with ones we think will be more acceptable, and we often rein in our creative idea—what results is a frayed remnant of creativity. The best way to coach yourself out of this is to recognize it when it occurs. When you hear yourself saying something like, "maybe I should just test the water with this more acceptable version," stop yourself from strangling your creativity. Once you do that, go back to the creative totality of your idea and launch it. You will find that nothing bad happens.

- **Deadlines.** We have to base our coaching on our relationship to deadlines. If deadlines dampen our creativity, there is nothing wrong with a little self-deception. Who does not use self-deception somewhere in their lives? We worked with a creative who could not deal with deadlines, so she moved them up by one week. She knew, of course, she was doing this, but it gave her a window to start "getting serious." The self-deception worked for her. We have another colleague who knows he has to wait until the last minute to be creative because he excels under pressure. Finally, we worked on a team with someone who believes in creative dreaming. If they could not solve their creativity problem any other way, they would take the last week before the deadline, and each night for that week, they would focus on the problem, go to sleep, and leave it to the subconscious to construct a creative solution. Find an approach that works best for you, so deadlines don't dampen your creativity.

- **Lack of boundaries.** If you have an enormous creativity deliverable, setting boundaries around it will be helpful. There is nothing more disheartening than being asked to solve a huge problem, and once you start, its size arrests you. One way to add boundaries is to understand your creative solution's limits, what it will not entail. In our work teaching people how to create and innovate within their organizations, we use an action-learning project as part of the process. When the class learns that they are going to be working with a local homeless center, their eyes get big and we can see the wheels start turning in their heads; without a word out of their mouths they are saying, "What? You want us to solve the problem of homelessness? This isn't what I signed up for!" At this point we tell them the problem of homelessness is too big for us to solve, but to trust the process because they are going to learn how to narrow down a big problem into a smaller focus and feasible problem that they can solve. We added boundaries to our homeless shelter work by exploring the onboarding process for new residents.

- **Too much focus.** This one is counterintuitive. If you find yourself overly focused on coming up with a creative idea, stop. Coach yourself to free up your unconscious, maybe by working on something else. Go for a walk, take a shower, do anything to give it a rest. You will be surprised when a creative idea pops up.

- **Fear of the crowd.** Remember that over-quoted axiom of how to get over your nerves in public speaking: Picture your audience naked. We will not go there for your self-coaching, but there is a kernel of an idea in this that we want you to consider. Who is the crowd? Who are these people who are judging you? Deconstruct the crowd and take away some of their power over you. Another notion is to reform the crowd. At your earliest opportunity, model the behavior that you would like when you pitch a creative idea. Reinforce a colleague who tries something new, who steps out into the abyss, or whose idea turns everything on its head. Show the crowd how you can compound creativity by taking someone else's idea and "Yes, and" it to a new compounded idea. "Yes, and" comes from the world of improv. Simply stated, when an ensemble member on stage delivers a line, your role as a fellow actor is to accept it, then add to it. In that way, you don't stop the action as it is unfolding. In a company setting, using "Yes, and" communicates that I accept your idea and I will add to it. Maybe the crowd is just waiting to be reformed.

- **Exhaustion.** We saved this for last because exhaustion is both a real thing and a constructed reality. If you are a mother of two, hold a full-time job, cook for your family, clean the house, and pay all the bills, by all means, it is a real thing. But ask yourself a question before you give into exhaustion. If you worked on the most interesting and self-rewarding creativity project, how much would you give in to exhaustion? Think of one of those creative times when you were so engaged you lost track of time. On the other hand, if you find you are working on a creative project that is not as enthralling and exhaustion creeps in, find small places in the project to energize yourself. It could be adding a learning element; it could be experimenting with a small creativity; or it could be working with a very creative person. We like to think of it as taking a creative lateral. Keep working on the project but find places where you can feed your creative curiosity. Often, we look back on the most creative experiences of our lives and wonder how we achieved them, how we found the time. The answer is that they were so engaging that we bent time and found the energy in our reserves because we knew the outcome would be more then we could ever have imagined. Reconstruct reality to find vitality in the things you love.

Now it's your turn. Use the "My Creativity Enemies List" exercise on the next page to identify what your creativity enemies are and how to overcome them.

The One Thing: The Creativity Boomerang

There are countless barriers to creativity. They span from what gets in the way of creativity within teams, to how companies willingly or unwillingly stifle our creativity, to the most significant barrier of all, ourselves. Any one of these barriers can minimize or stop our creativity, but more often it is a combination of these enemies that keep us from venturing out. Creativity is a gift that we can give to the world. When we do, it compounds as others add their creativity to it. Each person is unique and valued in how their creativity manifests. That's what makes the compounding work. There is a boomerang effect of creativity; once you unleash it into the world, it comes back to you in unimaginable ways.

🎨 Journal Exercise: My Creativity Enemies List

1. Create your enemies list. Brainstorm what gets in your way of being more creative.

Creativity Doodle

2. Select one of your enemies. Use the 5 Whys tool to get a deeper understanding of the enemy.

1.

2.

3.

4.

5.

Creativity Doodle

3. Reflecting on your answers to the 5 Whys, come up with a coaching experiment to help you overcome this enemy.

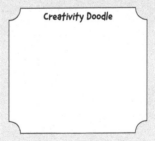

Creativity Doodle

We would like you to experience the boomerang of creativity. As you unleash creativity into the world, notice how it reaches others and how they react. Perhaps it was a song you wrote that helped someone through an unusually hard time. Or a story you told in a meeting that inspired someone to turn their life around. Or a process you innovated that saved people time so they could spend more time with their families. Or a hiring procedure you created that helped a long-underemployed candidate find a better job. Keep a lookout for the creativity boomerang. It may not always happen, but if you are lucky, your creativity comes home to you after other creatives have compounded it, after it has affected people in positive ways, and after it has left its gift on the world. When it does come back, it will astound and delight you. Fighting all the enemies will have been worth it because your creativity will come back in the form of love.

We've spent enough time looking at barriers, now let's migrate the question from "What's wrong?" to "How might we?" In the next chapter, we look at why creativity matters in organizations and particularly in talent development groups. We are moving from the boomerang of your individual creativity to the boomerang of an entire unit or organization unleashing creativity. At the organization or unit level, creativity can become a virtuous cycle that keeps moving toward an ensemble of people to unleashing their best selves.

PART 2

Creativity and Talent Development

CHAPTER 4

Why Creativity Matters to Talent Development

Making the simple complicated is commonplace. Making the complicated simple, awesomely simple, that's creativity.

—CHARLES MINGUS

The Face of the Customer

It was 2012, and Donna had been tasked with building a more ethnically and racially diverse workforce to better mirror the company's current and future consumer base. Appreciating that data has the power to provide insight, Donna conducted an analysis to fully understand diversity numbers for the cadre of universities where recruiting had been focused for the past five years. She quickly discovered that the current pool had racial diversity numbers in the single digits and at the primary university as low as 3 percent. She saw this as a "Yes, and" opportunity (which you'll recall is an improvisation technique that accepts a situation or what a person has shared). Donna realized she could use the approach to create space for building positive momentum to creatively address this problem. So, she proposed the continuation of recruiting efforts with the current pool of universities (*yes*) while casting a wider net focused on building relationships with smaller universities and colleges with student bodies primarily made up of people of color (*and*). During her conversations, she engaged with people who wanted to come alongside to think through new and different ways to engage potential candidates throughout the recruiting process and be willing to lead into the unknown. And throughout all her dialogue, presentations, and conversations with leadership, Donna made sure to share how this "Yes, and" recommendation was aligned with the organization's strategic architecture and firmly rooted in the organizational values of inclusion and diversity.

Donna's simple ask was to use a multiyear "try and see" approach by casting a net to build and nurture new and meaningful relationships, with a goal to create a more racially diverse and relevant workforce for the future. The ask to test a novel approach to address a complex challenge was met with a lackluster response by the university recruiting staff and leadership. "Relationships" with specific universities were a priority because of organizational politics and long-standing assumptions that these top-ranking universities were yielding the best diverse talent for the organization. Although the data spoke the truth that specific universities were not the right partners for building a more racially diverse workforce, decision makers determined it was best for recruiting efforts to keep the status quo. Taking the unknown journey to defy the crowd to build a genuinely diverse workforce was viewed as too big of a lift in light of other organizational priorities and available resources.

Something in the Water

> Creativity, as has been said, consists largely of rearranging what we know in order to find out what we do not know. Hence, to think creatively, we must be able to look afresh at what we normally take for granted. —GEORGE KNELLER

The two of us have worked a combined total of more than 35 years within a global Fortune 250 organization, where we experienced complexity everywhere. Globalization, mergers and acquisitions, organizational vision shifts, global recessions, the list goes on and on. Through the years, the seamless integration of people, processes, and systems to build efficiencies and save cost was an ongoing problem to be solved.

While environments at the local, regional, and global levels were inherently complex due to social, economic, and cultural attributes, this wasn't the primary challenge. The challenge was seeing smart, salt-of-the-earth people take a simple problem or issue and make it complicated. This happened for many reasons; perhaps internal politics, unconscious or personal biases, or underdeveloped leadership abilities were at play, or possibly they were simply making something complicated as a means to slow down the decision-making process. Often, people were not grounding themselves in the purpose, values, and strategy of the organization.

A clearly articulated, purpose-driven strategy is imperative. The purpose and strategy supported by the organizational values serve as an north star to guide people through complexity and keep the complicated at bay. A purpose-driven strategy and organizational values hold fast while the priorities of the day-to-day can and will fluctuate. As humans, we chart our course for the north star, based on what we know (using pattern recognition), consulting with thought leaders, and looking at future trends. The strategic planning process assesses for known risks and attempts to hypothesize for the unknown. Yet, there's still the opportunity for an unexpected event to charge in from out of nowhere.

We can all agree that the 2020 global COVID-19 pandemic would qualify as an unknown. This pandemic would halt the way we do business at local, regional, and global levels. Organizations with large, supportive infrastructures may have initially viewed their strategy as the north star, referencing it maybe two to four times a year. The issue is that they had lost sight of the purpose. The execution of the strategy had become almost rote. It was like an unconscious bias had developed. An inner voice was saying, "This is just how we do things. It's been working for us so far." When in actuality, people in the organization had become complacent. In the pursuit of operational efficiencies, it is not uncommon to lose sight of the whole system. It is easy to design the organization in a way where it relies on a select few or a specific department to be creative, think through the future, and ask, "what if?" Let's take a look at an example of an organization that didn't let complacency get in the way of a creative pivot.

Located in a refurbished buggy whip and corset factory, Journeyman Distillery in Three Oaks, Michigan, opened its doors in October 2011. It is one of those places visitors love to check out while they're vacationing in Southwest Michigan; it's also one of those places beloved by locals. Becoming known for award-winning whiskey, they were on a trajectory to continue to grow their business throughout the US. At the beginning of the pandemic in March 2020, Journeyman recognized a need. A primary weapon of defense against COVID-19—hand sanitizer—couldn't be found anywhere. With this recognition, Journeyman chose to shift its operations from distilling award-winning whiskey to manufacturing hand sanitizer approved by the World Health Organization. It was one of the first distilleries in the US to do so. Journeyman possessed the DNA to keep things simple, to pivot quickly, and to create. They didn't have an extensive infrastructure that came to a screeching halt. It was more like a pause; an intentional pause that gave them the space to view the situation's complexity and determine what kind of solution was within their span of control. They chose to ask, "what if?" What if operations shifted to distilling ethyl alcohol and mixing it with peroxide, glycerin, and water to manufacture hand sanitizer? Voila! A simple solution to address an immediate need during an extraordinarily complex time.

Journeyman's knowledge, skills, and mindset not only enabled them to manufacture a product and meet the immediate needs of the community; their ability to creatively address a challenge became a strategic advantage and differentiator for them in the marketplace, resulting in building and expanding upon an already loyal customer following.

Eventually, large organizations found ways to provide value to support the fight against COVID-19. However, the structure of these organizations and their sheer size ate up valuable time. It took time to analyze the situation, gain alignment on the best approach, and then retool processes, machines, and services.

Why share this story? The point is that there is a benefit for organizations to have the same DNA as Journeyman. Organizational design, talent management, and development processes must foster people's creativity to view and solve problems in novel ways every day. That way, when something unexpected comes from the left field, a creative mindset and the associated behaviors can fuel survival and, ultimately, organizational success.

What if an organization's purpose was something like, "We create products, services, and experiences so that people can thrive in today's world"? What if a primary driver of the strategy was focused on "We create." *We*—it's not *you*, *me*, or *someone else*, it's *we*. This focus creates a collective call to action, an expectation that people can and will be equipped with the knowledge, skills, and mindsets to be creative in their day-to-day regardless of their role.

Finding Your Inner MacGyver

Sometimes we can feel stuck when trying to see a new perspective or adopt a new mindset. This is where there is an opportunity to be like MacGyver, the 1980s TV icon. MacGyver worked with an agency devoted to righting the world's wrongs. And he had a knack for using everyday items and his creative wits to troubleshoot and solve challenges. For example, in season two, episode 19, his Jeep breaks down due to a leaking radiator. What to do? MacGyver grabs two eggs and cracks them over the radiator; the egg whites seal the hole, and he's off to save the day! The skill possessed by MacGyver is called *divergent thinking*. This is where a person looks at an item and chooses to find multiple uses for it that are unrelated to its intended purpose.

The good news is that this skill can be developed, and now it's your turn. Flex your divergent thinking muscle by working through the "Your Inner MacGyver" exercise on the next page.

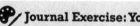 **Journal Exercise: Your Inner MacGyver**

1. In 45 seconds, list as many practical ways you can think of for using a paper clip. Sketch a doodle if you have the time.

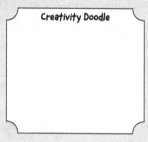
Creativity Doodle

2. How did you come up with your ideas?

3. How can divergent thinking be applied in your organization?

Complex vs. Complicated

We need rules to break the old rules and norms that otherwise we might bring to the creative process. —TIM BROWN

A purpose-driven strategy is intended to be the true north; competing and shifting priorities will always be part of our lives and organizations. If you're not currently working within a purpose-driven organization, we offer encouragement. You have a choice. You always have a choice in how you view a situation and how you choose to show up. Today, you can choose to view your organization as a creative opportunity. You can adopt a mindset to recognize the complex and identify what you can influence to keep things simple instead of becoming complicated.

Let's be very clear that there is a difference between something being complicated and something being complex. *Complicated* is linear; it can be diagnosed and solved and is usually a one-to-one ratio of cause and effect. *Complexity* is dynamic, interactive, and intertwined; it plays out at the systems level and is not necessarily at a one-to-one ratio of cause and effect. Here's an example of bringing these concepts to life.

There is high attrition among talent who have taken three-year developmental field assignments. Going into the position, they know that returning to headquarters is an expectation. However, once they move to the field to live, they end up establishing community roots; some may buy a home because it makes financial sense, and some meet and marry a partner. Some partners have substantial ties to the community and don't intend to leave. Upon completing their assignment, talent is advised about a development role for them back at global headquarters. The talent asks about other opportunities that would allow them to continue to add value to the organization and remain where they are. The standard response is that they were in a rotational development role and need to return to headquarters. If they want to grow and expand their career with the organization, working at the global headquarters is necessary.

So, is this situation complicated or complex? Take a look at ATD's Talent Development Framework, which identifies 39 different functions of talent development (Figure 4-1). Think about the puzzle pieces involved in this one scenario. At a minimum, compensation and benefits, workforce planning, talent management, succession planning, organizational effectiveness, and employee engagement are at play. Add the integration and coordination of these functions, and there is complexity. However, there is also an orthodoxy (a deep-held belief) that people must physically work at headquarters to progress in their careers.

Figure 4-1. ATD's Talent Development Framework

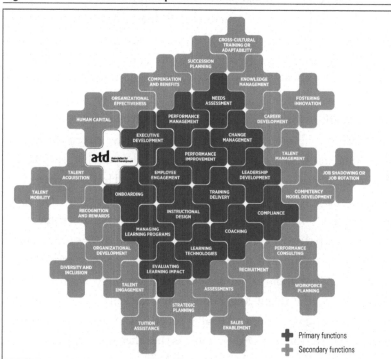

ATD and Rothwell & Associates (2015)

So, is this situation complicated or complex? We say it is complicated because of this orthodoxy—the deeply held belief that people must work at headquarters to progress in their careers. This situation could be kept simple by first recognizing that there is an orthodoxy. Second, challenge the deeply held belief by asking "what if," and work through scenarios where the effect is no longer the loss of talent but an environment that discourages their return. At organizations overflowing with people who feel valued, fulfilled, and engaged, talent does not unnecessarily leave.

People can learn to look at situations as complex or complicated. Once they determine the characteristics, this is where freedom begins. The psychological power in naming the situation opens up space for choice and freedom to create.

Creativity in the Chaos (the VUCA World)

Think about how our world is changing. As the saying goes, "The only thing certain in this world are death and taxes." Now, let's adjust this saying to be, "The only thing certain in this world are death, taxes, and change." Change is ongoing and inevitable; the challenge about change is the amount and the rate of speed.

As talent development professionals, it is our responsibility to ensure that the people in our organizations have the right knowledge, skills, and abilities to quickly adapt to and be resilient with frequent change. We know that training isn't the answer to everything (yes, we all encounter leaders who think this is still the case). We also know that training integrated within a holistic talent development process can be a game changer.

The training regimen for a person to become a US Navy SEAL is not for the faint of heart. It starts with a 24-week Basic Underwater Demolition/SEAL (BUD/S) training, followed by a 28-week SEAL qualification training program, but that's not all. Training for the first deployment can take up to 30 months. Adding all this up, a Navy SEAL goes through a minimum of 37 months of training.

In actuality, the SEAL program isn't just training; it is integrated into a much broader, holistic system of talent development. Through daily reinforcement (some may call it something else, but let's stick with this), Navy SEALs learn how to quickly adapt and remain resilient in pretty much any situation that comes their way. Adaptability and resilience are vetted out and reinforced so much that they become innate abilities, second nature.

Think back to pattern recognition discussed in chapter 2. Our minds look for patterns to simplify our lives so that our mental capacity is freed up to focus on more complex tasks. What if we took a similar approach to develop our talent? What if the knowledge, skills, and abilities to create were trained and were reinforced daily? What if integrating creativity processes and tools throughout all talent development efforts was a priority? Creativity can become the DNA of the culture and a way of being even if it starts with grassroots efforts.

The Talent Development Capability Model and Creativity

It's no surprise to you that we believe the potential to create is possible within every domain of the ATD's Talent Development Capability Model (Figure 4-2). The knowledge and skills identified for organization development and culture and for future readiness best align with what it takes to develop yourself and equip the organization to create.

We all know that there will be multiple starts and stops with projects that sit under the umbrella of talent development, from onboarding to performance management, to developing top talent for strategic succession planning efforts. Project success will depend on the level of sponsorship in the organization and its connection to the strategy. These projects' strategic focus may involve improving or creating scalable and repeatable processes to reduce risk or errors.

For some people, the word *process* is like fingernails on a chalkboard. They view processes as confining, and there is no freedom to create. To others, processes open up space to think about or do other value-added work and to create. The point here is that there is no right or wrong way

Figure 4-2. The Talent Development Capability Model

Building Personal Capability	Developing Professional Capability	Impacting Organizational Capability
• Communication • Emotional Intelligence & Decision Making • Collaboration & Leadership • Cultural Awareness & Inclusion • Project Management • Compliance & Ethical Behavior • Lifelong Learning	• Learning Sciences • Instructional Design • Training Delivery & Facilitation • Technology Application • Knowledge Management • Career & Leadership Development • Coaching • Evaluating Impact	• Business Insight • Consulting & Business Partnering • Organization Development & Culture • Talent Strategy & Management • Performance Improvement • Change Management • Data & Analytics • Future Readiness

to interpret the word "process." It is our responsibility as talent development professionals to be vigilant in scanning and reading the organization regardless of its function. We have a unique opportunity to choose to view the organization as a whole system, while recognizing that the system is comprised of individual parts. Complexity is also an innate part of the system. Creativity processes and tools are not enough to address the complexity and keep things simple. Individual people with differing life experiences, knowledge, and skills are also part of the system. Many parts are making up the whole. Efforts to build a culture of creativity will fail if diversity, equity, and a culture of inclusion and belonging is not a foundational component embraced by the organization.

> Even artists need a framework, an edge of the canvas, and this
> is what process does . . . it provides the edge of the canvas.
> —AMY CLIMER

The One Thing: You Have What It Takes

Creativity is like a bohemian patchwork quilt. It isn't meant to be perfect, and the edges aren't finished, yet it serves a purpose, such as the quilt shows love or serves as a tool for warmth. Before being assembled, pieces of material lie piled up, appearing mutually exclusive and not fitting together. Sewing a quilt takes patience, persistence, process, and being open to different perspectives. Herein we find four elements that make space available to create. The quilt's magic lies in the diversity of fabrics, textures, colors, and patterns. The color or pattern of one piece of fabric is highlighted when placed next to another material that brings out its best features. Each piece of fabric, once exclusive, becomes inclusive and now belongs together.

The beauty of having a culture of creativity is that the opportunity to create isn't constrained by or limited to one function, one person, or one point in time. Creativity is omnipresent, omnipotent, and resides in each one of us. Think back to what you read in the introduction and the four fundamental truths:

- Creativity is important.
- Creativity is inside each of us.
- We can learn to be more creative.
- We can overcome barriers to creativity.

We believe that you have what it takes to be creative and to do what it takes to develop yourself as a creative being as well as those around and throughout your organization.

The rest of the book will take you on a journey through stories, exercises, and reflection to:

- **Be curious.** A foundational skill for creativity
- **Be you.** Knowing yourself frees you up to be more creative in way that is uniquely you
- **Be with.** How to inspire others to be creative
- **Be-yond real.** Explore how creativity comes alive in our virtual world
- **Be more.** Leading yourself and others to recognize or generate ideas through novel perspectives that defy the crowd and create aha moments

CHAPTER 5

Be Curious

I have no special talents. I am only passionately curious.

—ALBERT EINSTEIN

Creativity is all about "bringing forth," and that requires action. A key element of creativity is curiosity. Curiosity is a superpower all of us have. Unfortunately, it's not uncommon for our curiosity to be buried due to inputs that shape beliefs about how we are supposed to show up, how we are supposed to act, and how we are supposed to "adult." Ultimately, fear of judgment, rejection, and not being enough can become inhibitions and kryptonite to curiosity. Even with the intent to be passionately curious, you can also unconsciously extinguish this desire. When this happens, your desire to authentically be who you are called to be and create in the way you are called to create just doesn't happen, and you can go through life and wonder, "How did I end up here?" But, our friends, the best news is that there is hope.

We're going to take a short journey as Donna shares a personal experience that has guided her perspective on how pressures shape who we are in our day-to-day lives. She is also going to share her thoughts on how curiosity can be resurrected or rediscovered.

Rediscovering Curiosity

First, let me start by saying that the experience I'm going to share with you profoundly affected my life. I decided to take a creative risk and disclose this intimate story for the first time in a public format. To be completely honest, I'm taking a deep breath as I write. My intent is to inspire and to make an impact in your personal and professional life, so much so that you take action.

Now for the story.

My father was a man of integrity; he was the quiet one in the crowd and what many would consider rather stoic. Dad was one to keep up on the local news and world events. He sought out ways to continually grow his knowledge in areas outside his vocation. I don't doubt that he knew that everything he was learning would serve him in some way at some point in his life. As a farmer, Dad was a master at repairing equipment, finding ways to make ends meet when it was a challenging year for crops due to lack of rain, too much rain, or any other unforeseeable act of nature.

Dad loved children, and they loved him because of the undivided attention, patience, and time he took in teaching them about the world around them. He found joy in being with them in their curiosity and wonderment; it was an opportunity to support their growth and development. I noticed that this wasn't always the same approach he had with some of his immediate family or other adults. I saw him be quiet and reserved when talking with certain people. There was caution with whom he would show emotion, whether laughter and joy or disappointment and frustration. The more I honed my knowledge and skills in talent development, coaching, and overall human development, the more I was curious about "why"; why Dad behaved the way he did. In 2006, I gained a little insight into some of the potential causes and effects of that "why."

I will never forget the 6:45 a.m. call I got from my mom on Saturday, September 30, 2006. Mom was driving home after spending the night at the hospital. She was calling to let me know that Dad had experienced a seizure at work. After multiple tests, he had been diagnosed with a brain tumor. I packed up a bag to stay for a few days and began my two-hour drive home.

The following day, I learned from the neurologist that my father had a malignant brain tumor positioned in the left and right frontal temporal lobes of his brain. The neurologist believed that he'd only had the tumor about a month and gave a prognosis of a six-month life expectancy. We were given treatment options and then sent home with the intent that Dad would return in a few weeks to begin chemotherapy and radiation.

The best-laid plans of mice and men often go awry.
—ROBERT BURNS

During a follow-up doctor's visit, we learned that the tumor was causing fluid and pressure to build up on Dad's brain. While the tumor was malignant and removal wasn't an option, Dad wanted to have as much quality of life as possible, and so he opted to have a craniotomy to remove the pressure from his brain. During the surgery, his surgeons discovered that he had also developed a neuro-generated condition that almost shut down his kidneys. Had Dad not opted for the surgery, he would have passed from kidney failure that very day. So, the surgeons first had to remedy this condition before they could conduct his craniotomy. Talk about an already complex experience getting more so.

Despite the stress and complexity of this entire situation, a very cool thing happened. As soon as my father woke up from his surgery, I experienced him doing things that I'd never seen him do, nor did I think he would! Just the day before, he was quiet and stoic. Now he was playfully shooting the occupational therapist with his resistance bands, and he was pretty talkative for a person who just had brain surgery.

A week after his procedure, he stumbled as he was getting up out of bed, and as I caught him from falling, he spontaneously danced with me. The irony of this action was that 15 years earlier, he had declined my request to dance with me at my wedding, stating, "Muffy [my nickname], you know that I don't dance."

My father, who loved to listen to music but never sang aloud, now spontaneously broke out into song. During this time, I learned that he used to love to sing and was part of the men's chorus in high school. One of my fondest post-surgery memories is our duet for the chorus of one of his favorite hymns:

I'll fly away, Oh Glory

I'll fly away;

When I die, Hallelujah, by and by,

I'll fly away.

If you're not aware, reasoning, judgment, and inhibitions are located in the brain's right and left frontal temporal lobes. I am confident that I learned this at some point; however, it never truly resonated with me. Here's a hypothesis I developed as a result of this experience. The pressures of the world had shaped how my dad behaved. In some ways, his desire to be curious or to create had become stifled because of inputs he had received throughout his life, and eventually, those inputs became inhibitions. The surgery had relieved pressure indeed. Dad no longer thought that he had to act a certain way because he was an adult. He was playful and ornery; it was almost as if he had been given permission to be a kid again.

Now for the point of sharing this story and its connection to curiosity.

We are all taught appropriate social norms and behaviors, or we learn them through observation. While having acceptable social norms and behaviors is designed to keep order, whatever that order may be, they can also become forms of pressure. The pressure to:

- add up to something
- speak a certain way
- act a certain way
- perform
- provide
- not fail
- not let people down

While a brain tumor was the cause of my dad's physiological pressure, he also had other pressures like those I just listed that built up throughout his 68 years of life. Intentionally or unintentionally, they became inhibitions that stifled his desire to emote, to sing, to play, and, in some instances, to be curious for fear of rejection or not being enough.

Here's the deal: You have a choice. First, you can choose to recognize that you are enough; no matter what others tell you, I know and believe that you are "fearfully and wonderfully made." You also have an innate cognitive ability to be curious and create, and we are all born with this ability. For whatever reason, my father didn't realize that he had a choice, or he didn't choose to change his perspective and recognize that he could play and emote with people other than children. I'm not going to psychoanalyze my father's situation, but what I can tell you is that he always had a choice, and so do you. Are you going to allow yourself to explore and not be restrained by thinking or saying "but," "I'm not," or "I can't"? Or, are you going to permit yourself to think, say, and explore the "what if" with eyes wide open to the possibilities?

Observe Curiosity Around You

Take a look at the children around you—in your home, outside your window, or on social media. Don't just give them a short glance; genuinely observe what you're seeing and hearing—if you truly stop and look, you'll see curiosity in action. Admittedly, curiosity in action can sometimes lead to undesired results, such as a toddler coming into the room with toilet paper stuck to their toes as a result of checking out the best color option of nail polish. Even still, it's incredible how curiosity naturally shows up. Children's brains are still developing—they are figuring out how to do things, subconsciously seeking patterns and connections to make sense of things around them.

In a 2014 article, Carrol Baker discusses ways to regain a childlike sense of wonder. As she notes, "Kids can be enchanted by simple things in the natural world that some adults would probably find a bit uninspiring or even ordinary: a midsummer storm, the mystical colors of a rainbow, even a tiny caterpillar scurrying up the garden path." Baker then goes on to share some thoughts from Australian clinical social worker Debbie Carberry, who believes that this unique mindset allows children to view the world with joy:

> In my job I sit on the floor with kids each day and they take me to a place where imagination knows no bounds. They'll pick up a rock and talk to me for 20 minutes about how beautiful it is or become enthralled by light sparkling through a window.
>
> It's all about perspective—viewing life through a lens filled with awe. When adults see a mud puddle, they'll worry about splashing mud on their new shoes to walk through it; in a child's eyes, a mud puddle is the perfect place to stomp their feet, to bury their hands in squishy, cool mud, and to make delicious mud pies.

Carberry's description is a fantastic example of curiosity in action.

What's the Point?

We are frequently asked, "What can be done to create or build a culture where people are creative and have the ability to think out-of-the-box? I need them to be able to look at and solve problems in different ways."

Here's the deal. The people asking these questions are usually in organizations that are keeping processes or systems in place that don't support the new actions and behaviors they are seeking from people. The pressure to meet time-critical objectives, the need to exceed stakeholder or shareholder expectations and deliver on metrics, and the rapid pace of shifting business needs and environmental variables are not going away. These established frameworks have served the organization well in the past; they subconsciously provide comfort in a volatile, uncertain, complex, and ambiguous world. In organizations where curiosity isn't a social or behavioral norm, a bias has evolved that a linear approach is the best way of viewing and solving problems. There's a perspective that allowing space for curiosity is time consuming and is reserved for people who work in a creative function or who are working on an innovation project. In other words, curiosity is fluffy and doesn't add value. While stakeholders may be pleased with the speed of execution to get to a solution, the impact on those working through the process is often overlooked to the point that some talent can become disengaged and uninspired. Diversity and inclusion are at risk because the focus is on getting a task done versus opening space for exploration.

So, what's the point? If we're completely honest with ourselves and with our organizations, shouldn't we be asking, "How do we build a culture where people are allowed to be curious?" and "How do we shift our processes and systems to enable curiosity within our day-to-day work?"

Choosing Curiosity

If you missed this the first time, curiosity is innate: We are all born with this ability. It is important to know and to remember that we don't lose our ability to be curious. While some people cultivate their curiosity through the arts and we're able to see or hear that art, other people cultivate curiosity through the experiences like building a business, starting a nonprofit, raising children, teaching, or developing talent. Curiosity is a choice, and it can be rediscovered or rekindled. It's about allowing yourself the opportunity to be curious and to create an environment where others can do the same.

Curiosity requires you to defy the crowd, whether that crowd is an external audience or an audience of one—yourself. Our encouragement is that you don't need a craniotomy to remove the pressure. You don't have to wait. You have a choice to:

1. Acknowledge the pressures.
2. Determine how pressures are serving you. Are they creating an environment where you can be curious and explore? Or have they become inhibitions that are now barriers to curiosity and creativity?
3. Choose to be curious and explore.
4. Take action to use your curiosity superpower to generate ideas about what's possible personally, professionally, and within your organization!

In her piece on adults and curiosity, Carrol Baker (2014) writes: "No matter what your beliefs, harnessing the childlike creativity you once owned so vividly can improve both your personal life and your work performance and prospects, making you more resourceful and innovative. American researchers Darya Zabelina and Michael Robinson carried out a US study in 2010 into adult creativity, asking adults to imagine themselves as seven-year-olds. They discovered that the more an adult acts and thinks like a child, the more imaginative and creative he or she becomes."

For this next journal exercise, let's take a cue from Carrol Baker and "regain a sense of childlike wonder."

Curious to Explore Another Resource?

Check out FourSight and the FourSight Assessment, born out of research by Gerard Pucchio, PhD, at the International Center for Studies in Creativity, Buffalo State University. The FourSight Assessment is an insightful tool that we use during participant-centered innovation and creativity experiences with individuals or teams. The assessment provides insight into preferences for creative problem solving within or outside an innovation process. What we appreciate about this tool is that it shines a light on how every person is naturally creative. FourSight is about the levels of energy throughout the creative process.

The One Thing: Expect and Respect Curiosity

You have the opportunity to relieve the pressure by allowing yourself and those around you to be curious. You have the opportunity to foster an environment where curiosity is expected and respected. You have a unique opportunity to defy the crowd and positively foster society and the world around us. Your internal and external voice can shape how you see yourself in the world and, ultimately, how you choose to show up.

Up next: Chapter 6 will take you through a process (which you will discover is not linear) and exercises to build a curiosity muscle—curiosity about you!

🎨 Journal Exercise: Childlike Wonder and Curiosity

1. Watch "Curiosity & Wonder" from PBS Kids or "Childlike Wonder" from TEDxUmeå by Caroline Ravn. Note which video you watched here:

2. Reflect on what you watched and list three to five key takeaways.

3. How can being curious serve you personally and professionally?

🎨 Journal Exercise: Childlike Wonder and Curiosity (cont.)

4. What do you want more of when it comes to tending to your curiosity?

5. List seven ways you can enlist your childlike wonder and curiosity.

1.
2.
3.
4.
5.
6.
7.

6. What action can you take within the next 24 hours to tend to your curiosity?

CHAPTER 6

Be You:
Inspire Yourself

 In chapter 5, we looked at curiosity and how it is a critical element of creativity. Now you're going to have the opportunity to apply your curiosity superpowers in the process of self-discovery.

Here's the deal: Creativity in talent development for individual fulfillment, employee engagement, and organizational success just doesn't happen; it requires engagement of the head, heart, and hands. Before you can expect others to be curious and creative, you've got to do the work yourself. It is foundational and critical that you experience and understand what it means to "defy the crowd." Not only does this give you the street cred of having gone through the process, but you are taking time to develop yourself.

Now, we know what you're thinking: "What? How can this be? Reflect and develop myself? When will I find the time?" We're always amazed at how the TD community does so much for the organization yet doesn't take the time to purposefully go through development experiences and actions for themselves.

Now is the time. You may feel a little uneasy, apprehensive, excited, and tingly, but that's all OK. This is exactly what happens when you take steps forward.

> Puzzles are like songs. A good puzzle can give you all the pleasure of being duped that a mystery story can. It has surface innocence, surprise, the revelation of a concealed meaning, and the catharsis of solution. —STEPHEN SONDHEIM

One Piece at a Time

We're going to make the creative process relatable by using an analogy of something we've all done at some point in our lives. Once you got the hang of this activity, you naturally figured out a strategy to take what could seem to be a daunting exercise and make it much more palatable by breaking it down into smaller organized tasks. We're asking you to think of creativity like putting together a 1,000-piece jigsaw puzzle!

Here are a few strategies for the process of putting together a puzzle, which in some ways are very similar to the process we will be discovering a bit later in this chapter:

1. First, you turn all pieces picture-side-up and spread them out. This enables you to see everything, even if the pieces don't make sense at the time. Having everything visible supports the desired end state. Your goal should not be to get through this chapter and all the tools in one sitting. Peruse if you must. Survey what the process entails and plan out your own strategy; however, don't let this chapter fly by without taking the time to assemble your puzzle. We want to be honest and tell you that this process takes time, but it is worth the investment—just like a puzzle.

2. Next, you sort pieces into groups and set aside edge pieces. In creativity terms, we call this "what you already know," and these may be what you call your boundaries. Then you begin sorting interior pieces into smaller piles based on the section of the puzzle in which they appear. This chapter's tools will support you in organizing insights you've gained from previous chapters and new information you'll gather throughout this chapter.

3. Now, assemble the border. At this point, you're starting to pull together the scope of what you need to accomplish. You're framing up the picture, or what some may call the guardrails.

4. Assemble the interior of the puzzle by sorting groups, colors, and patterns. Groups, colors, and patterns are really about themes, and you will identify themes as they show up throughout the

process. One thing to note is that some themes can be subtler and may not appear right away. Having a missing piece is totally fine; it's kind of like that one corner piece of the jigsaw puzzle that you can't find, and then one day, it miraculously appears.

5. Pay attention to piece shapes. The shapes of pieces tell the story of the connections as well as disconnections. The exercises throughout this book lead you to create and reflect on connections and disconnections. You've been attending to and building your observation muscles; in other words, how the different pieces are shaped.

Putting Together the Pieces: A Process to Evolve and Transform

A few things to note about this process:

- It is based on human-centered design, creative problem solving, creative thinking, and innovation processes.
- There are ample tools and techniques to leverage each step.
- The process is iterative, so as we like to say, "trust the process" —you'll get there.

Ultimately, our goal is to keep the process simple and relevant, so you can uncover insights and find something profound for yourself. And who knows, you may also share and apply the process or your findings in your role and organization.

The Creativity Development Process

You may be familiar with the phrase *creative problem solving*; while we appreciate this terminology, we're choosing not to use the word *problem* for this process. "Why?" you may ask. Well, we are using this process for development purposes and not strictly to solve a problem. We are addressing a challenge or area for development that isn't a problem but an opportunity. We are going with the appreciative inquiry route and saving the problem solving and root cause analysis for another topic and time.

Like in the other chapters throughout the book, we'll have tools to support you in exploring a concept. This chapter, however, will be a bit more prescriptive in that we're walking with you step-by-step through a process (Figure 6-1). The tools will even look a bit different than what you've experienced in other chapters. We're leveraging readily available resources for development. Thank you for continuing to trust us and trusting the process.

Figure 6-1. The Creativity Development Process

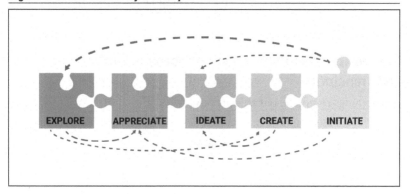

Step 1. Explore

You've got to start somewhere, just like the strategies for putting together a jigsaw puzzle, even if the final piece isn't what you expected and you don't end up being where you may have originally intended.

Explore is the first step. You can ask yourself, "What is the challenge I want to address?" In working with coaching clients identifying their topic of development, finding a topic with emotional resonance is a critical piece of the coaching puzzle.

Here's an example. A person states that they want to work on communication skills to support them in getting to their next role. That sounds like a great coaching topic on the surface level, so the coach and client march down the path of building better communication skills.

But after a few sessions, the coach notices that something is off with the client. Yes, they show up and they do the work; however, something is missing. They're going through the actions, but emotional energy and commitment aren't evident.

What was missing was an exploration of the underlying motivation for the request. If they had spent some time asking questions and not jumping right to action, it would have become evident that the client was looking to build their confidence. The topic of building confidence opens a broader space to explore. There could have also been opportunities to explore self-awareness, self-actualization, and countless other meaningful topics that would give emotional resonance and true meaning to developing better communication skills. Communication skills may still have been part of the action plan.

One of the social norms we have learned is that we need to get to results as soon as possible, it's ingrained in us to jump immediately to the solution. When we do so, the process becomes purely tactical, and it's almost as if we are unintentionally or intentionally saying, "Let's just get this done and over with, so we can move on." However, this misses the part of thoughtfully seeking to identify the topic and address or solve something more profound that will have a lasting impact.

We've all heard the phrase, "put a band-aid on it." Trust us, that's not the mindset to take with the creativity development process. Take the time to identify a challenge to address. Yes, it may take a little longer; however, the time spent up front is in the interest of having a viable solution in the end.

And some good news? As you go through the entire process, the challenge identified may shift or change. This is not uncommon. The thing to remember is that you need to start at the beginning—don't skip the exploration stage.

You'll also create "what if" statements in the explore step. "What if" is all about changing your perspective on a topic or situation—it's a technique that begins to shift your thinking to be about possibilities without being limiting or negative.

For example, I have received feedback about my ability to take over meetings when there is no clear purpose or desired outcome. While this is perceived as a strength of my ability to lead, I've also been told that I am missing opportunities to mentor and lead by example. So, that's an opportunity for me to ask myself, "What if I took the time to read the room a bit more before taking over a meeting? What if I identified someone else who could come alongside me to organize and lead the meeting?" This one question could then lead to other questions like, "How could it affect the leadership skills of others in the room if I took this action?" and "How might others be differently engaged with my new approach?" If you take time to thoughtfully work through the "'What If' Statements" exercise, you'll be better able to identify the challenge you'd like to address.

Now it's your turn. You may already be thinking of a "what if" statement for yourself, or you may be stumped on how to start. If you want some inspiration, here are a few examples of challenges to address using the "what if" format:

- What if I fell in love with a challenge instead of immediately jumping to a solution?
- What if I didn't have to have all the answers?
- What if I didn't feel stuck in the work that I'm doing?
- What if I viewed people as solution solvers versus problems?

If you need a bit more help to get going, you can also search online for self-reflection tools like the Wheel of Life or a personal SWOT analysis.

When you're ready, use the "'What If' Statements" exercise on the next page to come up with your own "what if" statements. Then you'll be ready to go further and deeper! Move on to Step 2: appreciate.

🎨 Journal Exercise: "What If" Statements

Use this space to write three to five of your own "what if" statements.

1.

2.

3.

4.

5.

Step 2. Appreciate

Now it's time to collect information or data through multiple sources and look at yourself through different lenses or perspectives. The key to this part of the process is to commit to being curious and not judgmental of yourself regarding what you are doing well or not so well. If that voice shows up with some negative comments, we encourage you to say, "Thank you for your input and trying to keep me safe or grounded. I'm going to ask that you step aside, and I'll let you know if I need any input from you in the future."

Remain as objective as you can be, and, we'll say it again, do not jump to any solutions. You now have an excellent opportunity to gather insights, clarify some things for yourself, and practice self-empathy. Let yourself be in the moment, sit with what comes up in this step, and appreciate what you've uncovered. You may or may not agree with or like what you've seen, heard, and experienced, or you may be delighted and very humbled.

Here's an honesty moment. We know that some of you want to move fast. You are solution and results-driven because this is the known expectation that has worked for you in the past. While we cannot tell you what to do or not do, we will highly encourage you to take anywhere from three to five days to go through this step. Give yourself time to gather additional insights about yourself.

"When I'm at My Best" and "How Might I (HMI)" are the primary exercises for Step 2.

When I'm at My Best Exercise

"When I'm at My Best" gives you permission to step out of your head to gather input from others for your own personal and professional development. In this exercise, you'll reach out to 10 people and ask each one to provide two to three words that describe you when you're at your best. *Note: You're not looking for a paragraph or even a sentence. Two to three words per person—that's it!* Then you'll write the words you gathered in a slot on your chart. Just one word per space. Once you've written out all your words, reflect on the themes that emerge.

How Might I (HMI)

"HMI" is an exercise for you to synthesize the insights you've gathered about yourself up to this point in the process and continue to frame up the challenge you're addressing.

If you haven't noticed, each step and tool you are working through is linked to or builds upon your previous work and this part of the creativity development process. In this instance, you need to go back to Step 1: explore, and review your "what if" statements. You also need to review the themes you identified in the "When I'm at My Best" exercise. Have this information in front of you because this exercise will help you synthesize the insights you've gathered, summon up your curiosity superpower, and create your "how might I" statements.

🎨 Journal Exercise: When I'm at My Best

1. Reach out to 10 people and ask each one to describe you in two to three words.

2. Fill in each space in the table with a word you've gathered. Create another page of tiles if needed—don't limit yourself to the tiles here.

3. Look at the words you've written down and reflect. Ask yourself:

What am I seeing?

What themes are emerging?

What is something that is causing me to be curious?

🎨 Journal Exercise: How Might I?

1. Choose a theme from the "When I'm at My Best" exercise that resonates the most with you and review its associated words. Write it down here:

2. Set a timer for 3 minutes.

3. Write as many "how might I" statements as you can using the format, "How might I _____ for/in _____ so that _____?"
For example: How might I build my confidence in working with senior leadership so that I can make a bigger impact in the development of manufacturing floor employees?

4. Review your options and choose one HMI statement that resonates with you to use in Step 3: ideate. Write that statement here.

A note of caution: Completing Step 2 does not mean that it's OK to jump immediately to a solution. You still need to find options to address your challenge. You are still working to gain clarity and appreciate the challenge you want to address. Step 3: ideate provides you the space to face assumptions you have about your challenge, expand options for solutions, and ideate about the possibilities.

Step 3. Ideate

Let's start with the fact that we strive to use no fewer than five ideation tools when we facilitate people through this part of the creativity development process. Why so many? Because ideation is all about looking at a challenge from multiple perspectives, breaking out or breaking through biases or assumptions, sparking insight, and freeing up space for thinking and creating.

In this book, we're keeping things simple and will only have you work through one ideation tool. If you'd like to use additional tools to expand your thinking and perspective, just do an internet search for "ideation tools," and you'll find plenty of options.

Now it's time for you to get to ideating on your HMI statement!

Opposite thinking is a great tool to use to look at a challenge from a new perspective and come face-to-face with your assumptions (Goossens 2020). If you're going to pursue bringing forth something novel, identifying different perspectives is a must-have for ideation and is non-negotiable.

For this exercise, select one HMI statement that you'd like to explore further. You'll use the "Opposite Thinking" exercise on the next page to identify and face some of your assumptions. To ensure you are challenging yourself to think bigger, broader, deeper, and differently, and that you have a surplus of ideas, you will work through this tool three times.

After you've completed the exercise, select one idea you have listed in the solutions column, which you'll take to the next step of the process—create.

🎨 Journal Exercise: Opposite Thinking

1. In column 1, write three assumptions you have about the challenge you are addressing.

2. Choose one of those assumptions to address.

3. Define at least two opposite realities in column 2 and reflect on how they affect the challenge you're addressing.

4. In column 3, describe a new service, offering, or improvement using the opposite realities you defined.

5. Repeat steps 3 and 4 for each assumption listed in the first column.

1. Assumption	2. Opposite	3. Solution
Describe an assumption you have about your challenge.	Describe two opposite realities of this assumption.	Describe potential solutions for your challenge.
	1. 2.	
	1. 2.	
	1. 2.	

Adapted from Goossens (2020).

Pause and Trust the Process

We want to take a moment and point out that while we've been guiding you step-by-step through the creativity development process, you may be seeing that it isn't as linear you initially envisioned. Look at the curved arrows in Figure 6-1 from earlier in the chapter—they illustrate where iteration typically takes place and that the process isn't truly linear but has movement and fluidity. It is important to revisit insights gained at each step for review and iteration, and to recognize how the linear-ness (yes, we just created a new word) of the process gets a bit hazy. Iteration gives some people a lot of energy, and some people feel slowed down because they just want to get to a solution and results quickly. It's usually during iteration exercises when we tell people to trust the process. The creativity development process isn't always a straight shot in getting from point A to point B; there will be a few pit stops along the way.

Step 4. Create

The create step is all about taking the ideas and creating a visual prototype. There are so many options for this step. You've been building your puzzle, yet the end picture still may not be crystal clear. You're at the step where all the pieces are starting to come together; however, the concept you started within your head may have evolved, and so you will now step back to create a refreshed or updated picture.

It's fun to explore and try different tools. The tool that resonates with you today may not resonate six months from now. Whatever tool you use, stay focused.

The create step aims to get a visual or line of sight to answer the questions about the potential solutions identified in the "Opposite Thinking" exercise. Potential questions include:

- What does the future look like?
- How am I going to get there?

To begin answering these questions, you're going to work through a simple exercise called "Letter to Future Self." This aims to bring a solution more clearly into focus for yourself and even how you talk about a solution with others. You'll want to be fully present, so put your cell phone on airplane mode. Physically relocate to a quiet spot that will allow you space to think and be for the next 10–15 minutes. When you are ready, settle into the space and calm your mind through two rounds of a breathing exercise.

Here's the process:

1. Close your eyes.
2. Take in a deep breath in through your nose for a count of four.
3. Hold your breath for a count of four.
4. Release your breath out through your mouth for a count of four.

Open your eyes, sense how you are physically feeling, sense how you are emotionally feeling. If you don't feel settled, go through the breathing exercise again. Once you are settled, it's time to craft your letter to your future self, using the journal exercise on the next page.

Give yourself at least 12 hours before moving to Step 5: initiate. Let the work you've just done marinate. You may think of a few more things to add to your letter that will bring even more clarity to what you have envisioned.

Step 5. Initiate

You've reached the final step! It's time to take action toward your solution, not that you haven't been taking any action up until this point because you have. You've gathered insights and distilled them into themes. You've explored the possibilities of what could be and created a vision of how things will be once your solution is realized. You have been iterating on your challenge through each step. The creativity development process gives structure and discipline to gain clarity on precisely what challenge is being addressed. We hope that you have gained clarity and that you have also fallen in love with the challenge and not a solution. When we jump immediately to a solution, we may find that we have addressed the wrong challenge and may have to deal with undesired consequences.

Journal Exercise: Letter to Future Self

Use the space below to write a letter to yourself six months from now. Think through these questions as you write your letter:

- Looking around me what am I seeing, experiencing, hearing, feeling?
- What has the journey been like?
- What do I know now that I didn't know before?
- Who are the people in my environment?

Once you're done writing the letter, use the space below to sketch a picture of what you see today and what you envision in six months.

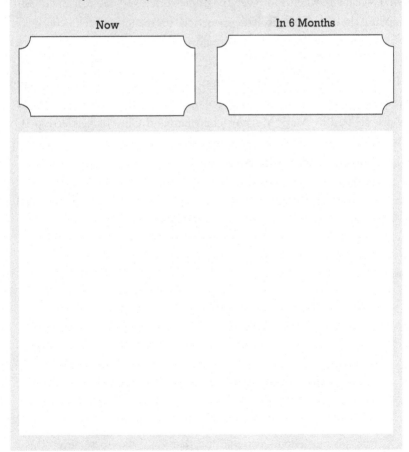

Now

In 6 Months

Now that you have clarity, it is time to pull together a plan of action for at least one solution you have identified. You may be thinking, "What kind of action plan is best suited for this situation?" Well, of course, we have some thoughts on this topic. Before building your action plan, let's look at the goal framework you will be using.

We assume that you're familiar with the SMART (specific, measurable, actionable, realistic, and timebound) framework used for input into a typical action plan. At the same time, SMART goals get to the point of who, what, and when. However, the framework is very tactical and doesn't tap into the emotional resonance beneficial for setting and achieving goals.

We've asked you to dig deep and to bring your head and heart to the creativity development process, and we're not going to stop now. To ensure the goals you are actioning against are emotionally resonant to propel and sustain you, we're going leverage the HARD goal framework created by Mark Murphy, chairman and CEO of Leadership IQ. We encourage you to use this framework as a litmus test for each goal you set and intend to achieve.

The HARD goal framework is:

- **Heartfelt.** "Is this a goal I want to achieve, or is it something I think I have to do because it's expected?" Heartfelt is all about resonance.
- **Animated.** Close your eyes and envision yourself taking steps to achieve your goal. "Can I see myself taking the actions needed?"
- **Required.** "What do I need to do? Who else do I need to include? What's my due date?" Required is tactical. If you can't easily identify or have a desire to figure out this piece, revisit your initial goal and determine if it is genuinely resonating with you.
- **Difficult.** "Too hard, too soft, or just right?" Difficult is a Goldilocks' moment: finding the right level of challenge that it's scary because you're shifting, but not so challenging that you're terrified or will quit.

Test this out; choose *one* solution that you'd like to achieve—this is now your goal. Take your goal through the HARD framework; if it meets the criteria, go ahead and create your action plan in the template provided in the "Action Plan" exercise. Go through this process as many times as needed to ensure you've identified a goal you will commit to achieving.

🎨 **Journal Exercise: Action Plan**

Goal:

Action	With Who	By When

Adapted from Credit Repair (2019).

Development is an ongoing journey, just like continuous improvement, and so you'll want to make sure that you incorporate opportunities for retrospective reflection. Think about it like this: You're going to look into your rear-view mirror to glean lessons as input for how you choose to move forward in your journey. Referring back to the work you've done not only in this chapter but throughout this entire book reconnects you with the perspectives and insights gained, validates progress made, and provides the fuel to continue moving forward.

The One Thing: Putting Your Creativity Process to Use

There's no one way for a person to develop and grow. It's not about taking a class, reading a book, having one-on-one coaching, or doing rotational work assignments. Development and growth are bigger—it is like putting together a puzzle. There is an end goal in mind accompanied by a strategy and process to put it together. The same applies to being creative. In this chapter, we have shared with you that there is a holistic process with supporting tools and techniques when you're looking to use creativity to address a challenge. You now have the experience to use this approach to create a new product or service or reimagine how the talent development function needs to operate in light of unforeseen social and economic changes.

We purposefully had you focus on yourself for the creativity development process. We hope you have the energy, curiosity, and hunger to learn more and explore how to engage and bring others into the conversation about what it takes to create. The next chapter will expand the space beyond yourself to explore what it looks like to inspire others to create and to defy the crowd!

> **You can't use up creativity. The more you use, the more you have.**
> —MAYA ANGELOU

CHAPTER 7

Be With: Inspire Others

One way to pay your creativity forward is to inspire others to be more creative. In this chapter, we will explore what might be holding others back from being creative. We want to impart three points of view throughout the chapter that can support you in inspiring others to be more creative and give you new ways to think about your creativity as a role model for others:

- Self-identify as a creative can vitalize your creativity practice.
- Lead your organization to reframe its environment to unleash creativity.
- Inspire creative habits in yourself and others as a key to lifelong creativity.

I Am a Creative, and I Inspire Other Creatives

> People learn their identities by projecting them into an environment and observing the consequences. —KARL E. WEICK

Ever wonder how we form our identity? One stream of research focuses on narrative identity; we create an identity by formulating our life experiences into an evolving internalized story that gives us a sense of purpose and authenticity in life. Often that story is validated by how the world reacts to us as we frame and reframe our stories over our lifetime. Within our narrative identity, some labels represent aspects of who we are: I am a mother; I am a runner; I am an accountant. A new inner narrative can reframe your self-perception and facilitate a path of self-led change. Take cancer patients who reframe their identity from victim to survivor, or those who struggle with alcohol who change their narrative to "I am a recovering alcoholic."

What does this mean for becoming more creative? At the start of some of our creativity workshops, we collect I-statements from participants about their creativity self-narratives. At the beginning of the workshop, these might include:

- I'm not the creative one on this team.
- I'm not very creative.
- I don't have a creative bone in my body.
- I am more practical than creative.
- My parents always said that my sister was the creative one.

We hope that during the workshop, their self-narrative about their creative ability will change. So, after a few opportunities for participants to experience how creative they can be, we ask them to write a proclamation of creativity. We strongly believe that if you are trying to change your identity, you should state it as a predetermined conclusion in the affirmative, then work on changing your self-narrative. In terms of creativity, with practice and intention, this can lead to a new self-identity.

Take a few minutes and reflect on your self-narrative about your creativity and your impact on others. Use the "My Creativity Proclamation" exercise on the next page to document your thoughts. Don't judge your statements; write them down without editing.

■ ■ ■

How hard was that to write? If you had a hard time, reflect on how that difficulty can sabotage your creativity. Next, we need to delve into what turns this constructed reality into an identity narrative, something that feels authentic. Let's start by looking at a few simple ways to find truth in your creativity proclamation, and if you are not already there, how to ease you toward the narrative: I am, and I inspire others to be creative.

✏️ Journal Exercise: My Creativity Proclamation

1. Capture your inner voice about your creative abilities and write them here.

2. Write in large letters: I am creative and I inspire creativity in others.
Draw some stars, arrows, hearts, and so on around it.

Creativity Doodle

3. Reflect on your reactions to your creativity proclamation and write them down. Does your proclamation seem true? Is it partially true?

4. Name your inner voice and write down what you want to tell the voice about your proclamation.

Fostering Creative Environments

Let's assume that your organization is not a design firm or a fashion house. If your organization is not creative, by charter, what are your choices to bring more creativity into your work? Worse, if your organization does not support creativity, how can you find a creative spot for yourself and others?

Two levels drive organizational performance. There is an extant level, level 1, which most people see and where we operate daily. Then there is the coded level, level 2, that is invisible to most of us.

Level 1: Extant

Level 1 drivers relate to the outcomes of the articulated behaviors compelled by your organization's vision, mission, strategy, and goals. These are reinforced in your company's daily operations, financial, performance management, talent, and leader systems. Level 1 performance drivers tend to be the most visible and the most well understood by everyone in the organization.

Level 2: Coded

Unknown to most, there is a secondary level. Level 2 takes the parameters and expectations of level 1 and codes them into the organization's infrastructure. Level 2 is invisible to all except those who are explicitly looking for it. Yet the coding level affects organizational performance as much as the extant level. Many of the protocols for level 2 performance drivers were put in place years ago. Often, they were not put in place to foster creativity; in fact, they were put in place to do just the opposite, ensure predictability, adherence to standards, and incremental and careful change. In short, it celebrates zero variance. This zero variance was written as a hidden code from the organization level down to the individual level in our job descriptions and performance assessments.

Suppose you want to change the performance of the organization and its employees to be more creative. In that case, you have to change the hidden coding that converts level 1 performance expectations to level 2. Often, as organizations adopt new strategies and ways of working, they neglect to address level 2 coding. This means they have level mismatch. One CEO described the mismatch this way: "It's like having a new strategy but funding the old one." Here are some examples of level 1 and level 2 mismatches.

You need to get to a meeting at 2 p.m. You borrow your friend's car and calculate that to make the meeting on time, by going 70 mph, it would take you 30 minutes to get there. You leave at 1:30, but once you get in the car, you realize that no matter how firmly and determinedly you press the gas pedal, the car won't go over 55 mph. You call your friend, who apologetically informs you that she has a teenage driver and set a speed limiter on the car to keep it under 55 mph. No matter how hard you try, you won't go faster unless you change the car speed limiter.

The same is true in organizations. One example is the stated need to have more people innovate (level 1) through small creative or innovation projects throughout the year. But the problem is that the budgeting system (level 2) does not allow funding for projects that are not planned at the beginning of each budget cycle. To change this, you would have to change the budgeting system to allocate small funds throughout the year.

Here's another example, which we refer to as "egg on our faces." We worked with an organization where level 2 coding undermined our creativity workshop. We were conducting creativity workshops, and, as usual, one of our ground rules was "everyone's ideas are valuable" (a level 1 aspiration). The tent cards for the workshop were printed from the company's internal training registration system. If you were an executive, the system printed your first and last name. But if you were an executive assistant, it had a coding (level 2) that only printed your first name. Let's call it innocent coding. But now it was not innocent; it was showing a delineation between levels and was chipping away at our ground rule that everyone is equal and valued. Welcome to invisible level 2, causing havoc on our best intentions in level 1. In this example you can also see an unconscious bias with level 2.

These are small examples, but the level 2 coding comes in all shapes and sizes. What they don't teach you in MBA programs is that if you want to transform an organization, you have to transform it at both level 1 and level 2. Most organizations skip the level 2 change. If you're going to support people to be more creative in your organization, training alone will not do it. If you are trying to inspire creativity in others, level 2 may wreak havoc on your best intentions. You have to look at level 2 performance drivers that may be limiting creativity and begin to adapt those so that creativity can be inspired and flourish.

Reframing Talent Development Organizations as Creative

As an individual in talent development, you can help your team identify level 1 and level 2 changes that need to take place to unleash creativity in your organization. Which talent development areas and practices is your team responsible for, and what level 1 and level 2 performance management drivers will make sure you can support and drive creativity at every turn? You will be able to inspire creativity in others by tweaking level 2 so that creativity will not be handicapped by organizational systems that are not creativity friendly.

Supporting Creative Habits in Yourself, Then Others

> You'll never change your life until you change something you do daily. The secret of your success is found in your daily routine.
> —JOHN C. MAXWELL

Habits are routines of behavior that are repeated regularly and tend to occur subconsciously. They become an automatic response to something. How can you make creativity a habit? If you study creative people over time, you can see not just their underlying process, but you begin to see their creative habits. Remember Asa, in the introduction? After years of practice, creativity has become a habit for her; now it emanates from her subconscious. How can we get to a place where we are creative without even thinking about it? How can you inspire others to form creative habits? Tim also has been working on making creativity a habit. He habit-stacked his analytic skills with creativity by developing a creativity checklist using the habit loop four laws, which we discuss next.

The Habit of Being Creative

Let's look at some compelling information about habits. We recommend *Atomic Habits* by James Clear (2018) as one of the best sources to understand how to create new habits. Here are three starting concepts to develop atomic habits:

- **Identity.** Clear's work recommends that we focus first on identity, not outcomes. Most of us say we will run a marathon, and then we put in place the goals and training needed. Clear recommends that we turn that around, start by self-identifying as a marathon runner. Having that self-narrative begins a different kind of change process that is longer lasting. It's a subtle but impactful change.

- **1 percent.** The term in the title, atomic, represents something minimal but of immense power. Clear asks us to break the behaviors we want to adopt into atoms, not grand sweeping declarations. Examples of what not to do are New Year's resolutions; we all know those rarely work. Over time if you work at the atomic level, compounding works in your favor. Additionally, atoms are easier to get our heads and hearts behind.

- **Systems.** Clear asks us to think about the systems that lead to the change, not the change itself. He has this great quote: "The score takes care of itself." Please don't focus on the scoreboard in a game; focus on the steps it takes to achieve the score, then the winning score will follow. If you are trying to keep your desk clean and tidy, merely counting the number of items on your desk will not lead to the outcome you want. What system can you put in place that leads to a neater desk? It could be a container system for all your pens and pencils, a mat to designate your computer area on your desk, a cord keeper to hide the cord mess. Identify the systems that lead to neatness.

Once you have considered these three concepts of developing atomic habits, Clear's work gives us the four laws of behavior change, which he calls an atomic-habit loop:

- **Cue: Make it obvious.** If you need to take a pill every morning and keep forgetting because it is in your medicine cabinet, make the drugs obvious by putting a pill beside your coffee maker, the first place you stumble to in the morning. This is about designing our environment around our cues.

- **Craving: Make it attractive.** If you are trying to get your basement painted and don't have the motivation, make it attractive. If you like to listen to audiobooks and can't find the uninterrupted time, use painting your basement as prime audiobook listening time. What constitutes a craving is very personal; what might be attractive to one person may not be attractive to anyone else.

- **Response: Make it easy.** We work with a woman who sleeps in her running clothes, so she is already dressed to go for her run when she gets up each morning. She does not have to go around and find her running clothing, risking giving up and eating a muffin instead. We move toward the path that requires the least amount of work.

- **Reward: Make it immediately satisfying.** Nancy makes her early morning swim sessions immediately satisfying by stopping afterward at a quirky local coffee shop to get a coffee. We work with a woman whose grandchildren live on the road next to her yoga studio. She stops off for a quick visit after her Shavasana.

Keep adding new habit loops by looking for the next 1 percent to gradually (atomically) move toward the new habits that form your new identity: *I am creative, and I inspire creativity in others.*

Applying Atomic Habits to Creativity

Contemplate using atomic habit loops as conducting mini-experiments to become more creative. As an example, say you want to be more creative in the many talent assessment workshops you attend. We found using Clear's atomic habits might work like this: Start by declaring your identity, not your outcome. Progressing toward that identity, you will have myriad mini-experiments leading to creativity as a habit. Each mini-experiment starts with a 1 percent change toward your identity and the systems you need to support it. You may have several mini-experiments before realizing you are creative as a habit, without thinking about it.

> **Identity: I am a creative person in talent pool workshops. I support others to be more creative.**

Now that you have an identity, use the information in Clear's work to form habits that make your identity your new reality:

- **Cue.** I will put my purple sharpie and sticky notes in front of me on the table at the workshop for everyone to see. If they ask what the supplies are for, I delight in saying: Just in case we have an opportunity to work on a creative idea together.
- **Craving.** Instead of telling myself, "I have to come up with an idea before this workshop ends," I say to myself, "This workshop will be better if I can add just a smidgen of creativity and get others to do the same."
- **Response.** If the opportunity arises, I will pass out the sticky notes. I will start by submitting one creative idea when there is a small opportunity and facilitate a "Yes, and" collaboration.
- **Reward.** I will put a star by the date of my meeting notes on my tablet when I offer an idea in a workshop and get through one "Yes, and" session. At the end of each month, I will reflect on how many stars I have added on my way to realizing my identity as a creative person and inspiring others in talent pool workshops.

I will discuss my creative work with my creativity coach and prepare for the next 1 percent creative habit experiment.

Use your wisdom and opportunities to create your own set of experiments. We find that people always get stuck when trying to set up their first mini-experiment. Don't worry; each experiment is as unique as you are, and there is no wrong answer. The secret is to be mindful of applying Clear's concepts to becoming more creative and inspiring others' creativity. Making the change is not a New Year's resolution; it comes down to atomic habits.

Work through the "Fostering Creative Habits" exercise on the next page to enable creative habits for yourself and others. Then you can start expanding out and exploring other ways to foster creative habits in teams.

Creative Habits Coach

You could also hold a team exercise to develop creative habits in others. Offer yourself up as their creative habits coach. Support their creation of and reflection on mini-experiments. Offer to support someone on your team as their creative coach on a one-on-one basis if you see them struggling to unleash their creativity. Additionally, hang out your "creativity habits coach" shingle and attract people to your new identity.

One Last Thing: Creativity as a Competency

This chapter covered how to inspire creativity in others, from creativity proclamations to facilitating or coaching creativity. The one area that we would like you to embed in your practice is to make a lasting change in the organization by instilling creativity as an ongoing competency. Remember that two levels drive organization performance. They are about a way of being and set of expectations that then become individual competencies with the ability to be more creative.

If you are trying to move your organization to be more creative, you also have to support the change at level 1 and level 2. No matter how hard you try to unleash creativity at level 1, level 2 will stop it, impede it, or

🎨 Journal Exercise: Fostering Creative Habits

1. Create an I statement about what aspect of creativity you want to develop as a habit.

2. Define the 1 percent and systems that might help you achieve the identity.

1 Percent	*Systems*

3. Use the four laws of behavior change to set up a habit loop.

4. After trying the habit loop for some time, reflect on your progress. What might be your next 1 percent?

Creativity Doodle

demoralize people unless it, too, is addressed. You can inspire people one-on-one as a coach and one-to-many as a facilitator. Still, you can inspire a whole organization to be more creative if you address the level 1 and level 2 performance drivers that lead to creativity from everyone and everywhere.

In the next chapter we look at the seemingly impossible task of helping teams be creative in the virtual world. While some things still work better in the face-to-face world, you will be surprised how much creativity you can unleash through virtual platforms. The key: using your 3D creativity to push the boundaries of what is possible while in a 2D world. If you dream it, it turns out you can virtually do it!

CHAPTER 8
Be-Yond Real

Organizations that do not use virtual teams effectively may be fighting an uphill battle in a global, competitive, and rapidly changing environment. Organizations that will succeed in today's business environment have found new ways of working across boundaries through systems, processes, technology, and people. They will make technology a valued partner in developing and delivering competitive solutions. —DEBORAH DUARTE AND NANCY TENNANT-SNYDER

Nancy and her co-author wrote the above passage in their book, *Mastering Virtual Teams*, more than two decades ago. It was the dawn of globalization, requiring creative collaboration across time and space. Virtual creative collaboration is not a new problem, but it has leaped from the purview of global companies into a new way of working and learning for everyone in less than 20 years.

Mastering Two Worlds

Joseph Campbell wrote in *The Hero With a Thousand Faces* (1949) about cultures worldwide that he studied. He found mythology in their storytelling that was surprisingly similar, even though many of the cultures were isolated from the rest of the world. Campbell described the story arc that all of the mythology shared as a departure, an initiation, and a return. The *departure* includes a call to adventure, a refusal of a supernatural aid, and crossing a threshold into new territory. The *initiation* includes a road of trials and, ultimately, a reward. The *return* includes a refusal to return and, ultimately, the hero becoming the master of two worlds.

This story arc is not unlike our lives in the heart of the COVID-19 pandemic. With COVID-19, we had a disruption in our world and a call to action to keep going in our working and learning lives. Many of us refused the call; we did not see how we could create virtually. We had a present-day supernatural aid in the form of technology as we crossed the threshold into working from the physical to the virtual world. In the initiation, we experienced trial and error, and ultimately most of us forged a working model for our virtual pursuits, a reward that we could fit to our needs. There was even some upside in the reward of not having to dress to go into the office. In the return, we refuse to go back to the way it was and, perhaps, will ultimately become the master of both worlds, creating a dynamic way of working between virtual and in person.

We can adapt the story arc from the hero's journey to tell our story of virtual workplaces over 2020. What will the mastering of two worlds be like, and how will our creativity shape it and be shaped by it?

We work with a very talented woman who is searching for a new job. After working virtually for eight months, she decided that she would never go into an office in her next job. We know CFOs running the numbers on the high cost of office space and planning for deep reductions in real estate. We, too, have spent the last many months in a virtual work and learning space, pushing the limits on how much creativity and collaboration we can get out of a Zoom window. We are living in the tension of the two worlds along with everyone else. We are not clairvoyant enough to predict the future; but we are betting on a *dynamic* world where virtual and face-to-face are blended and optimized. We don't believe we will see a world where no one ever goes into an office again, the work from anywhere model; nor a return to the old world where we only work face-to-face. With that as our premise, how can we use a *dynamic* approach to attract, select, evaluate, and develop talent? How can we use virtual platforms for creative problem solving? How can we win the war for talent and ensure what is best for our organizations and customers?

The Dynamic Delivery Model

In 2020, the world took a nosedive into virtual. Because of the pandemic, many offices had to close, leaving virtual as the only format to work, learn, and collaborate. As time went on, we saw some offices opening on a limited schedule, but virtual was still the communications backbone. As we look to the future, we see a blended platform for workplace creativity, task completing, collaboration, and learning.

For example, in the learning space, the first day of a workshop may be face-to-face to allow people to meet one another and discover how to work together. The middle part of the workshop may be virtual on a variety of schedules that suit our lifestyles. Then the last part of the workshop, to conclude and celebrate, may be in person. Virtual presents opportunities to beam people in when it would otherwise be cost-prohibitive or calendar-prohibitive. A workshop's keynote speaker may be virtual in the face-to-face portion. We are just beginning to stretch the potential of the virtual platforms at our disposal to make them work for us.

We see adding new permanent roles in organizations to accommodate virtual platforms: head of remote, virtual space curator, and virtual DJ. These roles require a blend of backgrounds in talent development, communications, and technical operations. They will be responsible for helping the organization use virtual platforms to achieve their outcomes. These roles will also be responsible for selecting upcoming platforms and working with beta versions to customize new platforms. They are technical facilitators or producers who ensure the virtual platforms meet the needs of the workshop participants and thus allow the content facilitator or leaders to focus on the content and messaging.

However, they are also crucial for designing workshops, because they have an in-depth knowledge of what the virtual platform can do. Increasingly, workshops are using multiple platforms simultaneously. This presents a teaching opportunity of getting participants comfortable using the new technologies without overwhelming them. We recently attended a workshop where the facilitator used more than a third of the workshop teaching the virtual steps required to perform one of the collaboration exercises. Clearly, she did not use her creativity to economize or normalize the time needed to learn the virtual platform.

After using virtual meeting and collaboration platforms for a period, all workshops seem to look the same and, as we get comfortable, our creativity begins to wane. Using our definition of creativity—*recognize or generate ideas through novel perspectives that defy the crowd and create aha moments*—you can use your creative skills to defy the crowd and use virtual platforms in new and unique ways.

A Virtual Working and Learning Inventory

When we convert our meetings, events, or workshops to a virtual platform, we often start with the virtual platform technology and what it offers—staying within its assumed limits. We suggest that is the wrong place to start. Instead, begin with your needs as a leader or facilitator and the environment you want to create, and then stretch and bend the virtual platform technology to meet those needs. When converting a face-to-face program, use your creativity to flip it to a virtual one. In addition to the agenda, slides, handouts, and other materials that need to be converted, use your creativity to transform the intangibles. These are the things we take for granted in a face-to-face meeting or workshop that are part of its success. Recently we were discussing this with a class, and a student said:

> What I really miss is taking in the whole person, observing their body language and seeing how they walk, how they enter the room, how they move around. I really miss eye contact, which is so hard to do on a virtual platform. I miss taking in the whole room and feeling the environment of the room. And finally, I miss the feeling of being together, working on something or learning something together in a space.

Before the pandemic catapulted us into a virtual space, we took all of this for granted. Of course, there are some advantages to being virtual that we did not have in face-to-face situations. One advantage is that speakers or faculty can be anywhere, opening the door to better availability of keynote or guest speakers.

Since we predict a blended approach that we are calling a Dynamic Delivery Model, let's look at what we know so far about collaborating virtually in terms of pluses and minuses (Table 8-1).

Table 8-1. Virtual Platform Collaboration Observations

Pluses	Minuses
• Meeting people in their homes; meeting pets; seeing another facet of their lives. (Although this only applies if they don't use a greenscreen background.)	• Meeting people in their homes can be invasive, especially for parents who are homeschooling and working, or people who live in confined spaces with roommates and are connecting from their kitchens (or bathrooms!).
• People are more prone to connect virtually given the hectic demands of our lives. It saves travel time.	• Internet connection can be a challenge. Rural areas may not have internet that supports video without immense lags. Or people may not be able to afford an internet connection.
• Everything can be saved and is on record.	• Buggy audio and video lag make it harder to for people who are hard of hearing to compensate by lip reading.
• 24-hour creative collaboration is possible if people work from different time zones.	• Can't take in the whole person because you only see what is above the desk. Assessing how they walk, sit in a space, or command or don't command a room is much harder.
• New roles are needed, such as head of virtual work or meeting producer. In real time while in delivery, roles are needed such as virtual DJ, raised hand spotter, chat scanner, and so on.	• Can't make direct eye contact.
	• Leadership intimacy is dead—the nuances (winks and nods) one gets from their leader are harder to see or nonexistent in a 2D space.
• Less expensive; no travel or lodging are involved	• Can't walk around as easily or discreetly during a breakout to see how people are doing.
• Getting facetime with leaders has changed, giving us more or easier access to leaders.	• The "getting-to-know" you dance is truncated in a virtual world. In a face-to-face world you maybe go out to lunch, but that's harder to do on a virtual platform, even with virtual happy hour.

Culture and Technology: Friend or Foe

Culture and technology can be your friend or foe in a virtual delivery of workshops. We had one workshop where most members came in 10 to 15 minutes late, long after we had assigned participants to breakout rooms. This can make the experience jagged for everyone involved, especially the virtual producer who has to jump through hoops to assign late participants to breakout rooms. In another company, one person in said that he was having trouble getting people to ask questions after his financial briefing in a Zoom meeting, and then it occurred to him to ask everyone to turn on their camera! Is your company's norm on virtual platforms to keep the camera off and use Zoom as a voice-only meeting? Do presenters turn on their cameras or leave them off?

Culture can play out in how different leaders or facilitators approach the virtual space. We occasionally work with other faculty or leaders who are not as willing to jump into new virtual platforms as we are. This makes for an uneven faculty delivery. In one case we worked with a leader who did not engage with the virtual participants; instead he read his lengthy comments, putting us all in a state of catatonic distress and causing some participants to surf their smartphones just below camera range. Working through these cultural preferences that spill over into the virtual space is something facilitators have to grapple with to ensure the best experience for everyone in the workshop.

On the technology side, the list of things to overcome is equally challenging. We worked with one organization where the virtual producer had what seemed like a 1990s era computer. She had many computer problems that kept the participants in limbo, waiting for her to solve her outdated computer problems in real time. We had another organization that had pre-pandemic controls on what virtual platforms their employees could use. By working with their HR, IT, and legal groups, we helped open up more opportunities for them to authorize new platforms, resulting in more virtual creativity and collaboration opportunities for their employees.

As a leader or facilitator, consider how your company uses a virtual platform and how culture and technology help or hurt your workshop objectives. As you are designing a virtual workshop, consider how many virtual orthodoxies your company has that you might have to challenge to ensure your talent development initiatives have the best outcome.

Knowing how culture and technology can help or hurt a virtual delivery, let's go back to the intangibles of a workshop. In addition to agenda, materials, content, culture, and technology considerations, we want you to focus on the intangibles that can be the x-factor in virtual meetings but that we take for granted or just assume will accompany a face-to-face meeting. We don't think about them until they are gone, a casualty of the virtual window. Intangibles help create an esprit de corps, establish community, and build teams. As you are designing your virtual workshop, how might you flip the face-to-face intangibles into virtual ones? In many cases, you have to work harder at virtual intangibles, even exaggerating them.

Use the "Flipping Intangibles" exercise on the next page to spend a few minutes listing the face-to-face intangibles. Then, pick one and flip it into the virtual space.

Using Creativity to Master the Dynamic Work Model for Talent Development

Talent development is a perfect world to learn how to master a dynamic delivery model. In the process of selecting, hiring, and acquiring, keep a journal of all of the different virtual platforms your candidates mention. Also, in evaluating new candidates, it's clear that those who show mastery in virtual platforms will be advantaged over candidates who do not. Finally, in the talent space, determine if you need a role that focuses on virtual applications such as a virtual producer or a service that can help you design and deliver virtual workshops.

No matter what topic you are covering in your workshop or meeting, here are 10 principles that can help—we call these the 10 Golden Principles of Virtual Workshops:

🎨 Journal Exercise: Flipping Intangibles

1. Identify a face-to-face meeting or workshop redesign for virtual.

2. List a few intangibles that contribute to face-to-face success now, before the virtual redesign.

3. Select one intangible and create variations on how you might flip it to your virtual platform. Think about ways that are not as easy face to face.

Creativity Doodle

4. Using the same steps, take each face-to-face intangible and flip it to a virtual intangible.

Creativity Doodle

1. **Maximize virtual time.** Use the time together to interact for collaboration and getting to know one another.
2. **Make use of pre- and post-time.** Expand the event by offering transactional tasks or new information beforehand in e-learning or other engaging formats.
3. **Move and energize.** Do not fall prey to becoming sedentary. Use creativity to get people up and moving.
4. **Overplay feedback and dialogue.** It's hard to read your audience, so plan multiple ways for them to give you feedback. It's also harder to have a dialogue. Emphasize both of these in your agenda.
5. **Create safe environments.** Work hard to make the virtual space safe.
6. **Change it up.** Use your creativity to keep people engaged, and attract them to the content.
7. **Remember the 10-minute rule.** Keep your instructions, talks, lectures, and presentations under 10 minutes. Virtual platforms make it easier for people to get distracted. Please don't read, engage.
8. **Limit to half days or less.** If possible, limit virtual workshops to four hours or fewer.
9. **Always practice.** While you might not have had to practice for your face-to-face events, you must practice for virtual events.
10. **Covert technology teaching.** Use every opportunity to microteach the virtual platform. For example, in introductions, give the participants a function to try. In the next exercise, add another function until they are confident in their use of the platform.

We have been moving toward this moment for a long time. The pandemic pushed us over the edge to all virtual all the time. As we move to the next phase of workshop delivery, we see a dynamic delivery model becoming the new norm—the mindful pairing of face-to-face with virtual delivery for an optimal user experience. The rules have not been written yet on how to do that. Use your creativity to push the limits of what is possible. Start with your outcomes and stretch and bend virtual platforms to achieve your results. The worst scenario would be to assume that delivering content in a virtual space is the same as face-to-face.

For talent development groups, the dynamic delivery model is perfect for attracting, selecting, evaluating, and developing talent. Also, talent development professionals are in an optimal space to lead the way on new dynamic models, given their continual boundary spanning work with multiple suppliers, companies, and candidates. Take this knowledge and put your creativity to work to deliver content and optimal learning and collaboration experiences for potential and existing employees and teams.

Let's look at a few ways you can think about defying the crowd and moving your virtual workshop to new levels of creativity.

We often conduct our creativity virtual workshops on Zoom, adding a collaboration technology such as Miro for posting ideas and brainstorming. While most working professionals gained experience with videoconference tools such as Zoom, Microsoft Teams, GoTo Meeting, Google Meet, or WebEx, due to the COVID-19 pandemic, very few use additional whiteboard or collaboration tools such as Miro or Mural. When you use these tools in addition to a videoconferencing platform, you run the risk of overwhelming participants, especially those who are not technology savvy. Additionally, participants may feel embarrassed if they can't use the tools as well as others. We addressed this by creating personas to understand their needs and then using the personas to add creative ways for participants to engage in workshop materials.

In a recent senior leader workshop, we started by developing a persona for the workshop team. In the process of creating the team persona, we learned that they are not very technology savvy. When they conduct Zoom meetings, they display slides and use the end of each presentation for Q&A. They don't use additional whiteboard tools to collaborate and brainstorm. As a result of our persona work, we realized that team members might be embarrassed because of their lack of virtual skills, so we took a creative approach to teach them the basics of the Miro platform we were using.

First, we asked them to introduce themselves using Miro. In the chat, we put the link to a Miro location, and when they clicked the link, they found themselves on a beautiful sunny beach. Once there, we asked them to introduce themselves using a sticky note tool to place their name on their spot on the beach. Posting is one of the basic skills that workshop participants need to know to use Miro. Next, we asked them to use a text box to type one word that describes themselves and place it next to their name. We were on Zoom and watching and talking to them while they worked through the steps. When they were not sure what to do, we shared our screen on Zoom to show them exactly how to solve the problem. Finally, we asked them to use the Miro tool that takes them to the internet to find the cover of their favorite album and post the graphic next to their names and descriptive word. In 10 minutes or less, they entered a new platform, introduced themselves, and used the three essential tools needed to collaborate in Miro. Plus, they had fun. As the workshop progressed, we used creativity to defy the crowd by introducing more complex tools. Without the persona work and pushing ourselves to be unique, we may have jumped right into giving out a set of steps, resulting in chaos and frustrating the entire team.

In another virtual workshop we conducted for bankers, we used our creativity to add music and dancing to the sessions. We started each day asking a different member to tell us their song of the day. Throughout the day, we played participants songs at breaks or during other times when we were not in deep conversation. Some members gave us songs from other countries. It was fun and inclusive. By the end of the workshop, we asked participants to dance. With a bit of encouragement, they got out of their chairs and danced to the songs we played. Once we started with music, participants opened up and suggested other creative ways to engage. One woman asked everyone to change their Zoom name to reflect a hidden skill. We found that when you model creativity in a virtual space—mainly when you defy norms—it opens up the flood gates by giving others permission to be creative.

Use your creativity to defy the crowd and add new and unique ways to engage your virtual audience. When you do, you might be surprised how willing others are to use their creativity to join in to make your workshop something new and exciting.

The One Thing: Technology Follows Outcomes

As we move forward in the virtual space, the rate of change for technology will be mind-boggling. It is important to start your virtual events with the outcomes you are trying to accomplish, not whatever the latest technology that everyone is using. If you start with what you are trying to accomplish, you can find the best technology to suit your outcomes. If you work in an organization that selects technology for you, you can do the same thing but at the feature level. Once you determine your outcomes, you can stretch and bend the technology to meet your needs. In architecture, form follows function. In the design and delivery of virtual programs, technology follows outcomes.

In the next chapter, we look at how you can lead others to be more creative. You'll see that you can use the creativity development process from chapter 6 not just to help yourself be more creative. You can also use it to unleash creativity in others.

CHAPTER 9

Be More: Lead Others

Every child is an artist, the problem is staying an artist when you grow up. —PICASSO

Much of this book has focused on how to move your creativity to the next level. The notion of defying the crowd is helpful as a clarion call to overcome our inhibitions. If we look at team creativity, it has all the components of individual creativity, but with a kicker: The team *is* the crowd. The peer pressure that team members feel not to stand out is sometimes heightened in creative work teams. The question is how, as a leader, you can support team members to flip the *fear* of the crowd to *embrace* the crowd. How can you support teams to reclaim creativity that has been lost to them since childhood?

In this chapter, we'll review six leadership requirements for maximizing creativity in teams. Then we'll apply the creativity development process to teams. Last, we'll delve into designing work environments for creativity.

1. Keep an Eye on the Prize

Start teams with a clear and straightforward picture of the outcome and how it will link to the organization's strategy. This may require you to take steps to operationalize your unit or organization strategy. Start by getting your hands on it. This seems relatively simple, but is often a more significant task than you imagine it should be. Organizations often do not have a strategy, have the strategy in pieces, or have a strategy but the employees of that organization are not aware of it.

Even though it is not your job to find the strategy, doing so will pay dividends for the creativity of your teams. Restate the strategy in simple terms everyone can understand, get it on one page, and become an agent for the strategy. We often recommend creating a strategy map, like the one discussed in a *Harvard Business Review* article more than 20 years ago (Kaplan and Norton 2000). Use your good judgment on how to create a map. If your organization is sensitive about its strategy, and many are, be sure to involve the key players when creating the map or reviewing it, even though that may take more time. You don't want to trigger the immune system. Start creative teams with the strategy map and use it to keep them going in the right direction. Encourage them to link how their project will help with strategy execution. Also, demonstrate how the strategy offers a broad space for creativity but also has boundaries.

How does this relate to creativity in teams? If you are skillful as a talent development leader, the team you lead will become widely creative. There will be times in the process that your team will diverge and think bigger and broader than you might have thought possible. Please don't stop that process. At some point, the creative team will have to converge. For example, they may have 10 creative ideas to work on but only the bandwidth and budget for one. Help them use the strategy map to prioritize their work. *They* must be the one to prioritize, not someone else, and to do that they need to have a good understanding of your organization's strategy. The key is not letting the strategy curtail the team's creativity, but keeping a tether to reality.

2. Model the Behavior You Want

There are some truths to leading creatives to consider. If you want something from others, demonstrate it first. If you want others to be creative, demonstrate that. Take time not just to be creative but to include the team in your creative process. Be open about failure and discuss how you deal with it when you put yourself out there and your creative idea or project does not make the cut. Give your team insight into how you use creativity in other parts of your life, not just at work. Be vulnerable and share your experience of going through the exercises in this book. Take the time to participate as an equal in the team's training and creativity work. It is detrimental to creativity to have people who are observing or sitting on the sidelines.

3. Remove Team and Individual Barriers to Creativity

Review chapter 3 and its list of barriers to creativity. Work on a plan to eliminate or reduce team creativity barriers. Additional team barriers include:

- **Informal team leaders who diminish creativity.** These people might not be formally assigned the role of project leader, but they hold sway over the attitudes and behaviors of everyone else.
- **External factors that overwhelm teams.** These include organization downturns, senior leadership changes, strategy changes that deemphasize your team's charter, or members of other groups who might be disruptive to your team.
- **Team makeup changes.** When you go from a period of team stability and then key members change, it can throw a wrench in your creativity processes.
- **Lack of leader support.** Senior leaders may, accidentally or on purpose, "put-down" your team's creativity. They might say, "You need to get practical; we don't have time for pie-in-the-sky dreams."

4. Embrace Diversity, Inclusion, and Acceptance

Creativity happens at the intersections of things that do not normally go together. In the case of team creativity, this manifests itself in the need for all types of diversity. As a leader, continually strive for diversity in thinking, backgrounds, levels of the organization, race, gender, lifestyles, preferences, and groups from outside your department, business unit, and organization.

One way to add diversity to your team is to invite new members, either core or SMEs. And you can address inclusion by making sure each new team member is onboarded and paired with an existing member.

Getting to know your team members beyond the immediate task will also allow everyone to bring their whole person to the group, not just the part that they think other team members will accept. You can honor areas of their whole person (that they are willing to share) by inviting them to share or lead an excise that might coincide with their background. Mostly, model the behavior you want. If you as the leader are inclusive and accepting, your team members will follow. You can also create inclusion exercises where you help the team decide what is and is not OK for the team culture.

5. Create an Ensemble Mentality in Teams

As a leader, it is not enough to invite diversity; the team members have to feel and behave as an ensemble. *Ensemble* comes from the theatre world, where a cast of actors help each other, have each other's backs, and never leave another member hanging. Ensembles are the equivalent of giving each team member unconditional support. Often a good way to get teams to experience the power of an ensemble is through improv training.

6. Encourage Playfulness

Study after study shows creativity and playfulness are not just related, they are positively correlated and predictive. Playfulness enhances creativity. Playfulness is the quality of being light-hearted, not worrying about competence or being self-important, and not taking norms as sacred. People who are playful are fun to be around; they are uninhibited. Playfulness as a trait fits nicely within our definition of creativity as defying the crowd.

As a leader, this means two things: upping your game in playfulness and figuring out how to bring playfulness into team activities. There is a great deal of research about adult playfulness. For example, the Adult Playfulness Trait Scale, created by researchers Shen, Chick, and Zinn (2014), reports playfulness traits that enhance creativity. The traits are fun, belief, reactivity, uninhibitedness, and spontaneity.

Playfulness is a crucial trait in creativity and leading creativity. Use the "Playfulness" exercise to reflect on the playfulness you can bring to opportunities. Remember to think about your playfulness orientation and how you might increase your playfulness in creative endeavors. Playful traits include starting and enjoying fun activities, being uninhibited, not fearing being seen as silly, and being spontaneous.

✋ Journal Exercise: Playfulness

Describe a time you added playfulness to a work activity that resulted in more fun for your colleagues. Then draw a cartoon of yourself in a playful mood.

Creativity Doodle

Describe the most uninhibited person you know. How does this help them be more creative? Then draw a symbol that will help you remember to be playful.

Creativity Doodle

Now that you have some insight into the key behaviors you should demonstrate as a talent development leader to encourage team creativity, let's look at how you can make creativity a team process.

Leading and Facilitating Teams Through Creativity's Highs and Lows

Creative tension and output can manifest in predictive behaviors as creative teams mature. If we look at the creativity development process from chapter 6 and apply it to team stages of maturity, we see a recurring pattern of highs and lows (Figure 9-1).

Figure 9-1. Creativity Development Process for Teams

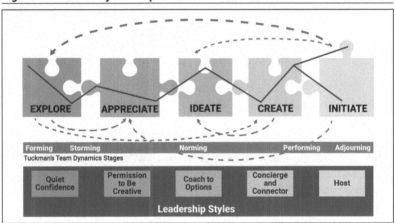

Explore: Quiet Confidence

In the explore stage, individuals come together as a team and start considering how they will work together. Psychologist Bruce Tuckman's model of team dynamics calls this is the forming stage. Most teams start on a high, excited to be on the team and work on something creative. However, it does not take long for the fog to set in as they tussle with the path forward and how they will collaborate. As a leader, the appropriate leadership style is to add as much structure as the team needs. The team realizes that this is uncertain terrain, so displaying confidence and offering structure in the form of a team process will be beneficial.

A talent acquisition team that we worked with was looking for a creative solution to assess new talent in the innovation space. In the explore step, the team created a sandbox to gather opportunities. A sandbox gives creative teams the boundaries of where to play. In this case, the team decided that they wanted to explore how potential MBA recruits collaborate with existing employees to solve an innovation problem. They wanted to see how the applicants collaborated with existing employees and how they used their innovation knowledge to enroll others versus arrogantly solving the problem.

Appreciate: Permission to Be Creative

Appreciate is a challenging stage for creative teams. The creativity tools in this stage are usually new to team members, and they might be hesitant to be creative. Examples of creativity tools in this stage include orthodoxy tools, analog tools, and nominal group technique. This stage is an adaptive problem-solving stage with no right answers. Often teams feel like they are in limbo or not sure they are headed in the right direction. This stage is often called the storming stage in group dynamics.

The appreciate stage is where team members become frustrated or reorganize how they want the project to go. This is often the first stage where one puts their creativity to work in the team. For healthy, creative teams, this is where they start relying less on the leader and begin to find their way with distributed leadership. As a leader, an appropriate style here is to "give them permission to be creative." Encourage them get over that initial hesitancy to go outside the box by encouraging them to be creative, modeling creativity, and supporting their creative muscle building.

The talent acquisition team decided that they wanted to try something new. They wanted to form teams of new MBA applicants and existing employees and give them an existing innovation problem to solve. They named it the Company Innovation Challenge. As we watched them move through this stage, they struggled. In the beginning, they kept asking us to solve the problem, but as they progressed, they quit looking to us and made some decisions on their own. These decisions centered around how this might work and what the innovation problem should be. For example, is it new to the world or an incremental problem? Is the innovation's timeframe months or years? They had a few disagreements until they came together with a path forward. They created what they called an opportunity brief with the team size, employee names, a problem definition, which innovation tools would be used, the amount of time for the development evaluation, and the location.

Ideate: Coach to Options

By the ideate stage, the team is in the thick of it. They are dividing and pursuing their quest for insights and possibilities. This is also the stage where new people might join for varying lengths of time to add diversity and know-how to specific streams of creative ideation. In group dynamics, the team might still be in storming but should move into norming as they begin to see what is possible. The appropriate leadership style in ideate is to support the team to stretch and create options. For example, leadership questions might be: Is that the biggest this idea can be? What can we group it with to make it more creative? How might we . . . ?

At this stage, the talent acquisition team divided themselves into smaller task groups: planning communications to the applicants, identifying the location and tools needed for the exercise, and identifying a company sponsor to introduce the innovation challenge to the team. They were starting to work well together and trusting each other. They also supported each subteam in being creative and thinking outside the box.

Create: Concierge and Connector

In the create stage, the team will begin to find their stride. They will be making hard decisions about what initiatives might move forward. They enter the performing stage, although some teams may revert to storming as decisions are made. Some team members may think that their ideas were not advanced. Most of the create stage sees the group's creativity move from intangible to tangible as they begin prototyping and testing. The appropriate leadership style here is as a concierge and a connector, introducing members to people, teams, or companies that can assist them in the initiate stage. This might also be where you find the things they need: people, funding, technology.

The talent acquisition team started to fine-tune their innovation challenge. They ran into some dead ends but quickly rebounded and took new paths. They could even create a budget and a senior leadership brief to communicate to key people in the company how the innovation challenge was going to work and what they were looking for in the applicants.

Initiate: Host

In the final stage, initiate, the team's creativity leads to an outcome. This stage is also where the team disbands. The group dynamic stage is adjourning. As a leader, the appropriate leadership style is as host. Team members will leave the team with a different perspective on how the team did as a whole, as well as their individual performance on the team. This is an opportunity for you to meet with each member one-on-one and help them get to their next assignment. It is also a time to help them reflect on the team results so they might take lessons-learned to their next creative team.

■   ■   ■

These descriptions are generalities. Each team has a unique character and culture. What is common is that creative teams will go through ups and downs, and your role as a leader is to pivot your style to enable the team to move into the next stage. Being aware of the different team stages and how the team reacts to each stage will help you in your leadership of creative teams.

The talent acquisition team hosted their innovation challenge. The results were outstanding. The company not only benefited, but the MBA applicants commented that it was one of their favorite assessment tools they had experienced at any company. Their experience made them want to work for the company. The team selected the successful candidates and communicated their choices to the hiring supervisors so that offers could be made. In their last meeting, they commented on how rewarding it was to work together and how sad they were that the assignment ended.

Designing Environments for Creativity

As a leader, a great deal of your time helping teams become more creative will be spent creating an environment where creativity can thrive. We want to look at how to do that through designing six types of spaces that cultivate the best creative experience for your teams.

The Physical Space

The physical space can support or hinder a team's creativity. While most of us cannot make sweeping changes to our physical space, small, playful details can add a spirit of creativity. For example, post quotes around the room that relate to creativity. Add fidget toys or tactile objects to help inspire teams when they are creating. Dividing the space into workstations helps too, especially if you have a large area. We facilitated a creative team where we had part of the room set up in round tables. The teams sat at the tables when we had new information and new materials to present—this was the presentation space. We set up the second half of the room in creative vignette spaces with whiteboards, sticky notes, and a printer to print graphics—this formed the collaborative space. Physical spaces that support movement are ideal.

When you are designing the physical space, think about the outcomes you are trying to achieve. We suggested to one leader who wanted to communicate their first creativity team's journey and spirit with the rest of the organization that they set the team up in the cafeteria, so everyone would walk by them on their way to get a coffee. Or their curiosity would be inspired as they interacted with them when they were picking up lunch. What communal or common spaces can you adapt, repurpose, or redesign to bring out creativity in your team?

The Virtual Space

Many creative teams work in a virtual space. In chapter 8, we outlined how to host a virtual creative team. Be mindful and intentional when you set up virtual spaces. Think about the theme you want to create and use your virtual options to contribute to that theme. Additionally, blend the physical and virtual spaces for optimal outcomes and experiences.

The Safe Space

We suggest a planning session targeted solely at creating a safe space. It is important to make safe space planning a deliberate act and not leave it to chance. For example, we strongly suggest that you do not record your face-to-face or virtual sessions. Recording always plays havoc with people's willingness to go all-out creative.

When someone takes a risk, big or small, be sure to acknowledge that risk so that others will see that they can do the same. Something as little as allowing people to pass in a creative exercise when it is their turn connotes a safe space. By allowing them to pass, they know that they will not be embarrassed.

The setting of ground rules also adds to a safe space, especially if they come from the participants. Confidentiality is vital. If team members believe that any crazy idea they post will be talked about outside the team, they will be less willing to be creative. Asking to hear from those who have not had a chance to speak is another way to create a safe space, especially if it is an open-ended query, so as not to embarrass someone by calling on them.

The Ensemble Space

From the first day, encourage the team to create an ensemble space. This is where we practice the kind of ensemble skills that stage actors use.

Teach and promote the use of "Yes, and," where an idea is meant with an instant yes, then the receiver adds to the idea. Use exercises to demonstrate that ensemble members have one another's backs. If someone steps out, the team supports them. In the same token, team members have accountability to help each other look good. That means that if someone is struggling, other team members jump in to help, with no judgment.

One good "Yes, and" exercise is storytelling. Have participants stand in a circle or give them an order of who follows whom in a virtual space. Start the story with one line and make it provocative. For example, "Jack woke up from a deep sleep and panicked when he realized that his expensive watch was no longer on the dresser beside his bed." Then ask the next person in the circle to say "Yes, and," followed by a new line for the story. Go around the circle until everyone has had a chance to add to the story. The team creates a story on the spot. It works because they can't really think ahead and simply have to accept and add on to the last line. One note for leaders if you try this: Remind the team that they are in a work setting and to make sure the story is workplace appropriate.

The Equality Space

Creativity requires equality. If you want teams to excel at creativity, everyone must be respected and on equal footing. If people on the team hold roles in your organization at different levels, encourage everyone to leave their titles at the door. We worked with one team where, when members suggested ideas, they glanced over at the senior person in the room for approval. We worked hard to eliminate that counterproductive behavior. We have had people actually write their title on a sticky note and place it on the outside of the door to remove that sense of oversight from superiors.

The Experimental Space

One of the best things you can do to enhance creative teams is to add the mindset of experimentation. This means that we can say or do things and then take them back. This also means that if a member wants to try something, they can have some space to test ideas without everyone having the ability to shut them down. Simply normalizing being able to say "I just want to experiment with this" is liberating.

■ ■ ■

As a creative team leader, consider these six spaces and dial each one up or down to fit your needs. The space around a team is paramount to the creative pursuit of a solution. None of these spaces has to add cost or time to your project, so experiment with them and keep adjusting until you get the creative space that your team needs to excel.

People Are Agents of Their Creativity

The most successful creativity team leaders encourage people to become agents of their creativity. Provide members with the skills, tools, and knowledge to create and judge their ideas. It is much better for a team to realize that their creative idea should not go forward than to have a senior leader stop their idea. This can often have unintended consequences for creativity. If you give teams the information and knowledge of how the organization or customer will judge their idea, it is to their advantage to evaluate the idea for themselves.

We worked in a company where the senior leadership identified three criteria for a creative products, services, or processes. They took the criteria and added a self-scoring mechanism to each team's toolkit so, at crucial decision points, they could self-evaluate how they were doing or if their idea would be funded. Having that self-scoring mechanism served two purposes: it educated teams on what it took to get their idea the green light and it allowed teams to be the agents of their ideas. Using this criteria as the basis, they could pitch to leadership why their idea should go forward, they could adjust their creative product, service, or process, or even shelve it if it did not pass muster. With the criteria and scoring in their hands, they did not need a panel, board, or senior leaders to tell them why their creative idea might not go forward.

The One Thing: Playfulness

We cannot emphasize enough how important it is for leaders to develop a sense of playfulness when leading and facilitating creative teams. We work with all kinds of leaders and facilitators. We notice that those who have a higher playfulness quotient get more creativity out of themselves and their teams. After taking the Adult Playfulness Trait Scale, we recommend looking for activities and workshops that help you develop playfulness in the areas in which you want to expand. One good place to start is to take an improv class. Look for other experiences that unlock your playfulness; we know it is in there dying to get out.

Epilogue

What has been will be again, what has been done will be done again; there is nothing new under the sun. —ECCLESIASTES 1:9 (NIV)

Some may consider the opening quote of this chapter to be pessimistic and uninspiring. And yet, the statement is true, isn't it? Think about it. What events and experiences in your life or in the lives of those around you are *really* new and have never happened before? Isn't it better said that these things are new to *you*?

Here are a few examples to get you started in your reflection:

- While 2020's COVID-19 pandemic felt unprecedented (and in some ways it was), we can look to prior pandemics such as the 1918 flu as precursors.
- For those who remember *The Brady Bunch*, the opening theme showed the main family members in a three-by-three grid visual. That's kind of like our now ever-present Zoom or Microsoft Teams meeting.
- What about trends in reclaimed wood furniture? Here people are taking the old and making it "new."

While these examples demonstrate "there's nothing new," it doesn't mean that creativity is no longer an option.

The beauty of creativity is that it is endless because, as humans, we continue to evolve. Throughout the book, we have shared examples and stories of people who chose to be curious and explore—looking at what is seemingly unconnected to uncover insights and gain a fresh perspective, to consider or see something in a different way than they had at first. We shared tools and techniques for how to go about seeking fresh insights or perspectives. We challenged you to test known biases or uncover unconscious biases—those that shape what you think of yourself, your organization, and the world around you. We had you explore pressures that influence how small you choose to be versus embracing the superpowers that are uniquely you!

As we went through our creative processes to find resonant words, stories, and exercises, you were consistently at the forefront of our minds. Building personal capability, developing professional capability, and impacting organizational capability are not skills that are generated overnight, and we know that the work can be both very tough and very rewarding. We wanted to create a space where you felt inspired, challenged, and psychologically safe, so you would take the steps and make choices to explore yourself and the world around you through different lenses. We hoped (and continue to hope) that you were willing to embrace the messiness that creativity brings.

As co-authors, we committed to each other to challenge ourselves, our intellect, perspectives, biases, and innermost beings through this experience. While this book's vision and intent is to support your ongoing growth as talent development professionals and humans, we want the same for ourselves. We chose to respect and trust each other and the creative process. We discussed moments of those voices telling us to "stay safe" and be comfortable with what we know and not take a creative risk to call forth something more significant or profound. Together, we actively built a safe environment for authentic and real dialogue that ultimately gave freedom and a voice to what you have read and experienced.

May you go forth with:

- Broadened insights, knowledge, skills, and behaviors about creativity
- Confidence and competence in what it takes to identify novel perspectives, recognize opportunities to create, and then generate ideas and solutions

- A personal relationship with what it means to defy the crowd and the courage to continue your journey of creativity

■ ■ ■

Without courage, there can be no creativity. —GEORGE PRINCE

All the best to each of you; feel free to connect with us on LinkedIn and let us know how your journey is going.

—Nancy and Donna

Appendix:
The Creativity Journal

We have long believed in the power of journaling, both unstructured and structured, using text and graphics. The structured journal pages in this book are designed to help you more deeply relate to the creativity concepts we've introduced. Many of the exercises also ask you to draw a creativity doodle. If you're not used to drawing, you may be hesitant to start, but once you do, you'll find that doodling gives you a different way to communicate your thoughts. The combination of text and graphics creates a fuller picture of your idea. Defy the crowd and jump in.

While we embrace technology, we still see the value of varying creative approaches. We know there are many apps and technology solutions for journaling, but we prefer to the transformative power of writing and drawing on a piece of paper. It gives you time to think and contemplate, and it creates a symbiotic space for reflection. It also allows for something that apps often limit, the evolution of a page. You're able to see how your thoughts evolved by looking at everything you've crossed out, drawn over, and written sideways in the margins. Keep this in mind as you're working through the exercises—you don't want them to look edited, typeset, or permanent.

As Nancy's Italian friends and relatives say about stop signs—the journal structure is just a suggestion. Feel free to change the format to suit your own needs and draw outside the lines. We've included these completed versions only as thought starters or for inspiration. Remember, there are no right answers!

🎨 Journal Exercise: Your Creativity Muse

My muse: Jiang (from the talent pitch)

1. How did they demonstrate creativity?
Did their creativity touch on these parts of our definition: recognize, generate, novel perspectives, defy the crowd, aha moments?

I was on a talent intake team that had to pitch to senior leaders. Jiang threw out the idea that she could sing the conclusion using a fun rhyming verse. No one had a better idea, so we agreed.

Creativity Doodle

the new powerpoint

2. Why does this example resonate with you?

I was terrified! No one sings to senior leaders. I moved away physically and emotionally. I wanted to keep my options open in case it did not work. But it worked really well and I felt like a coward. How hard would it have been for me to commit!

Creativity Doodle

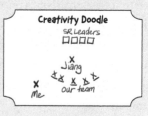

3. What are your takeaways either about how to demonstrate creativity or how it affects you when you see it?

1. Go the opposite direction, but you have to commit to it.
2. When I agree to a new idea, I need to overcome my fear and go with it.

Creativity Doodle

Norm →→→→→→
New Norm 〰〰〰〰→

Yes, And go for it!

Journal Exercise: Jobs to Be Done

What three things will you hire creativity to do? In the spaces below, write out and sketch your concepts.

Example 1

At work, I am part of a team that's redesigning talent selection. I will use creative tools to bring in new perspectives. I will hire creativity to have my colleagues see me in a different light.

Creativity Doodle

Example 2

My eight-year-old daughter is bored in some of her classes. I will hire creativity to create new ways to attract her to the material.

Creativity Doodle

Example 3

I volunteer on the board of our local soup kitchen. We need new insights to get funding. I will use creativity to lead differently.

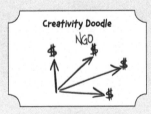

Creativity Doodle

🎨 Journal Exercise: "What If?"

1. Write a short paragraph about a current situation you view as a challenge or problem.

My industry is changing and I am acutely aware that I need to either:
· Change careers
· Adjust or expand my current skill set to become more marketable within my field

2. Now, reframe the challenge or problem as an opportunity by writing one "what if" statement.

What if I give up entrepreneurship and instead become an employee?

3. Write three additional "what if" statements about the same opportunity.

1. What if I try something new or learn a new skill set, but it doesn't pay off?

2. What if I find something completely different that fulfills me more?

3. What if what I am called to do isn't lucrative?

4. What's it like for you to see the previous challenge or problem as an opportunity?

Frightening! The idea of breaking from my pattern seems reckless.

5. How will you incorporate "what if" into your thought processes and conversations within the next 24 hours?

I will journal, research possibilities without judgment, and be open to my findings.

🎨 Journal Exercise: My Most Creative Team Experience

1. Think back over the teams you have been on, in any capacity (work, volunteer, personal). Select the one experience you think was most creative.

The talent development team where we took the new company values and created a learning map and work-team experiences for every team in our company.

Creativity Doodle

2. Describe and sketch what you and others did to make it so creative.
Did you break the norms and go to new spaces? Did you apply a new idea or technology? Did the team have a deep creative experience that bonded the group? Was there a creative sage in the group that helped everyone be more creative?

We scanned the world to find new technology and then adapted it to our application. It was a lot of hard work, but the result was worth it.

Creativity Doodle

3. Describe and sketch the feelings of being in that group.
Think back on how you felt at the most creative time for the team. Note your inner thoughts and feelings.

Free, high performing, satisfied, curiosity, happy

Creativity Doodle

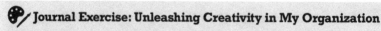 **Journal Exercise: Unleashing Creativity in My Organization**

1. Brainstorm the top three creativity barriers in your organization.

· It takes too much time to work creativity into projects
· We have a shut-down culture that intimidates creativity
· We don't know how to be creative

2. Pick one that attracts you. If you collide it with creativity, what intersections arise?
For example, if not enough time is the barrier, the creative insight might be how can I make more time? One intersection that emerges is that everyone has discretionary time at work. Think about how to attract those who want to use their discretionary time on creativity.

Time: Create rapid creativity tools, use creativity attraction to tap into people's discretionary time, attract those who want to be creative.

3. How might you bring these solutions forward to help unleash more creativity in your organization?
You might start a Pints and Pencils affinity group or monthly creativity events in your department. Your solution will depend on your organization's traits and how much you are personally willing to invest in it.

Start a creativities affinity group. Experiment with a Pint + Pencils Event.

Journal Exercise: My Creativity Enemies List

1. Create your enemies list. Brainstorm what gets in your way of being more creative.

- Don't know the tools and terms
- Feel like creativity cannot become a habit-I can't rely on it
- I don't have time to waste on creative endeavors without an outcome
- I don't like being judged

Creativity Doodle

2. Select one of your enemies. Use the 5 Whys tool to get a deeper understanding of the enemy.

No time to waste without a clear outcome:
1. It makes me not want to try.
2. If I put a lot of time into it and nothing great comes out, it's wasted time.
3. I don't like to waste time.
4. I have way too much to do.
5. I don't prioritize well.

Creativity Doodle

3. Reflecting on your answers to the 5 Whys, come up with a coaching experiment to help you overcome this enemy.

Prioritize 30 minutes each morning to be creative. Give yourself permission to wonder or to not come up with something creative. Call it creative restorative time-think about it like meditating.

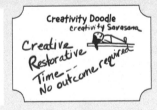

Creativity Doodle

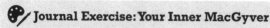 **Journal Exercise: Your Inner MacGyver**

1. In 45 seconds, list as many practical ways you can think of for using a paper clip. Sketch a doodle if you have the time.

- Hold papers together.
- Pick a lock.
- Poke a hole in the syrup top.
- Hang a picture on string.

- Clean a small space.
- Hold up a climbing vine.
- Make a bracelet.
- Hang an ornament.

Creativity Doodle

2. How did you come up with your ideas?

I've done all these things.

3. How can divergent thinking be applied in your organization?

Taking an expected process and looking at it to see if it's the most efficient process. Maybe it is—but over time, experience and technological developments suggest it probably can be improved or simplified.

Journal Exercise: Childlike Wonder and Curiosity

1. Watch "Curiosity & Wonder" from PBS Kids or "Childlike Wonder" from TEDxUmeå by Caroline Ravn. Note which video you watched here:

"Curiosity & Wonder" from PBS Kids

2. Reflect on what you watched and list three to five key takeaways.

· Curiosity starts by slowing down. Taking time to see and smell.
· Be present.
· There is always more to a situation, person, or object.
· Kids aren't self-conscious.

3. How can being curious serve you personally and professionally?

· Less inhibitions   · Delve deeper   · Better retention
· More confidence   · Better connection   (memory)

4. What do you want more of when it comes to tending to your curiosity?

Connection   Whimsy   Aha moments

5. List seven ways you can enlist your childlike wonder and curiosity.

1. Listen to my son's conversations with his friends.
2. FaceTime my young nieces and talk, listen, and play with them.
3. Go for a slow nature walk. No time limit!
4. Take my son to a museum and let him guide me.
5. See a Cirque de Soleil performance.
6. Go camping and leave my phone and computer behind.
7. Teach art to elementary students

6. What action can you take within the next 24 hours to tend to your curiosity?

Listen to my son while he plays with his Legos.

🎨 Journal Exercise: "What If" Statements

Use this space to write three to five of your own "what if" statements.

1. What if I change careers?

2. What if I adjust or expand my current skill set to become more marketable within my field?

3. What if I spent time developing my fine art skills?

4. What if I started to network through my local chamber?

5. What if I spent more time marketing myself?

Journal Exercise: When I'm at My Best

1. Reach out to 10 people and ask each one to describe you in two to three words.

2. Fill in each space in the table with a word you've gathered. Create another page of tiles if needed—don't limit yourself to the tiles here.

Focused	Positive	Determined
Energetic	Happy	Focused
Determined	Curious	Thoughtful
Happy	Independent	Determined
Determined	Confident	Energetic
Enthusiastic	Focused	Detailed
Funny	Energetic	Focused
Independent	Creative	Confident
Positive	Positive	Aware
Independent	Open-minded	Positive

3. Look at the words you've written down and reflect. Ask yourself:

What am I seeing?
Several people had similar responses, particularly around focus and determination.

What themes are emerging?
There seems to be a sense of high energy, independence, and focus.

What is something that is causing me to be curious?
I appear to operate with intense drive when I'm at my best. Friends, family, and co-workers deem my "best" to be when I'm producing.

🎨 Journal Exercise: How Might I?

1. Choose a theme from the "When I'm at My Best" exercise that resonates the most with you and review its associated words.

Determined

2. Set a timer for three minutes.

3. Write as many "how might I" statements as you can using the format, "How might I _____ for/in _____ so that _____?"
For example: How might I build my confidence in working with senior leadership so that I can make a bigger impact in the development of manufacturing floor employees?

· How might I use my determination to identify the next steps in my career?
· How might I focus my energy to explore ways to add creativity and human interaction into my daily work?
· How might I trust that my sheer dogged resolve will result in a successful outcome if I just give myself the space and time to pursue a change in career?

4. Review your options and choose one HMI statement that resonates with you to use in Step 3: ideate. Write that statement here.

How might I trust that my sheer dogged resolve will result in a successful outcome if I just give myself the space and time to pursue a change in career?

🎨 Journal Exercise: Opposite Thinking

1. In column 1, write three assumptions you have about the challenge you are addressing.

2. Choose one of those assumptions to address.

3. Define at least two opposite realities in column 2 and reflect on how they affect the challenge you're addressing.

4. In column 3, describe a new service, offering, or improvement using the opposite realities you defined.

5. Repeat steps 3 and 4 for each assumption listed in the first column.

1. Assumption	2. Opposite	3. Solution
Describe an assumption you have about your challenge.	Describe two opposite realities of this assumption.	Describe potential solutions for your challenge.
Will take too much time.	1. 2.	
Won't make enough money.	1. 2.	
Will require additional schooling or certification.	1. Could make more money. 2. May not need to make more money.	· Minimize my expenses in preparation. · Do my research and thoughtfully take steps that are fiscally responsible. · Define a clear financial plan and stick to it.

Adapted from Goossens (2020).

Journal Exercise: Letter to Future Self

Use the space below to write a letter to yourself six months from now. Think through these questions as you write your letter:

- Looking around me what am I seeing, experiencing, hearing, feeling?
- What has the journey been like?
- What do I know now that I didn't know before?
- Who are the people in your environment?

Once you're done writing the letter, sketch a picture what you see today and what you envision in six months in the space below.

Now	In 6 Months

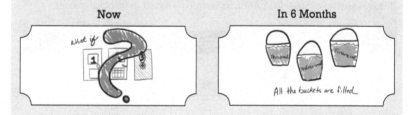

To Me,
This can be summed up in two words: TRUST YOURSELF. You've never started something you didn't finish and have never encountered something you wanted and could not achieve.

Six months from now, you'll be trying something more fulfilling than what you're doing today. You'll be exercising your creative skills in a much more forward facing way. You'll be doing work that is more meaningful and impactful to others.

You'll look back on today and wonder why it took you so long to trust yourself and your ability to make things happen when you put your mind, heart, and hands to it. History has proven that you will succeed.

I look forward to experiencing the change and opportunity as they present themselves.

🎨 Journal Exercise: Action Plan

Goal: To alter what I'm doing professionally to have a greater impact on people while better using my creativity.

Action	With Who	By When
Join a professional networking group.	My local chamber	This week
Become more active through social media.	LinkedIn or Twitter	This month
Create a space for creative development (a studio).	In my home office	Two months

Adapted from Credit Repair (2019).

🎨 Journal Exercise: My Creativity Proclamation

1. Capture your inner voice about your creative abilities.

- If others lead, I can be creative.
- I'm never sure if my creative ideas are good.
- I have some creative examples I am proud of.
- I helped my co-worker come up with new ideas.

2. Write in large letters: I am creative and I inspire creativity in others.
Draw some stars, arrows, hearts, and so on around it.

Creativity Doodle

I AM CREATIVE *and*
I inspire creativity in others!

3. Reflect on your reactions to your creativity proclamation and write them down. Does your proclamation seem true? Is it partially true?

I'm not sure I am there yet—but I'm getting closer!

4. Name your inner voice and write down what you want to tell the voice about your proclamation.

"Comfy Couch": Thank you for keeping me safe and comfortable over the years. I've realized that I need to be in a place physically and mentally that will support my creativity. I'm inspired by the fact that I inspire others, and I want more of this in my life, and because of this, I need to let you know that I'm finding a new supportive place to sit.

🎨 Journal Exercise: Fostering Creative Habits

1. Create an I statement about what aspect of creativity you want to develop as a habit.

Creativity Team Facilitator: Out-of-the-box thinking

2. Define the 1 percent and systems that might help you achieve the identity.

1 Percent	*Systems*
We will create one impossible dream before we start solving the problem.	· Out-of-the-box creativity tools · Inspiration examples of impossible dreamers

3. Use the four laws of behavior change to set up a habit loop.

· Cue: We will add a call for impossible dreams before we start problem solving to our team ground rules.
· Craving: Recap impossible dreams accomplished by our organization. Our team has a strong need to "wow" people.
· Response: We will put the team into dyads and use the impossible dream tool to create an out-of-the-box idea per team. Then we'll vote on the most out-of-the-box idea (fun voting).
· Reward: The winning team will get an "Impossible Dream" sticker (or other fun prize).

4. After trying the habit loop for some time, reflect on progress. What might be the next 1 percent?

The first two attempts were OK-people stayed in their comfort zone. On the third attempt we had some fun with it and a few great ideas emerged. Next 1 percent is to use great idea nuggets in our solutions-put our ideas to work.

Creativity Doodle

IMPOSSIBLE DREAMS

🎨 Journal Exercise: Flipping Intangibles

1. Identify a face-to-face meeting or workshop redesign for virtual.

Design Thinking Workshop for Talent Acquisition Team

2. List a few intangibles that contribute to face-to-face success now, before the virtual redesign.

- Quickly getting to know people
- Reading body language of workshop participants
- Building a community that continues after the workshop
- Using coffee breaks to get to know one another
- Evening dinner for light discussions and fun

3. Select one intangible and create variations on how you might flip It to your virtual platform. Think about ways that are not as easy face to face.

Building community:
- Breakouts with new people each time
- Fun introductions exercise on whiteboard
- Change your window name by adding an adjective; Nancy (movie buff) Tennant
- Chat your biggest learning in the workshop
- Create a playlist for the waiting room

Creativity Doodle

Community Campfire

4. Using the same steps, take each face-to-face intangible and flip it to a virtual intangible.

- Getting to know people: Start the session by asking about the story of your name.
- Reading body language: Check in periodically, asking people to chat how they are feeling.
- Coffee breaks: Find an app for impromptu meetings between two random participants
- Evening dinner: Virtual happy half hour.

Creativity Doodle

🎨 Journal Exercise: Playfulness

1. Describe a time you added playfulness to a work activity that resulted in more fun for your colleagues. Then draw a cartoon of yourself in a playful mood.

I dressed in costume to dispense information about the upcoming office Christmas party, even changing my manner of speech and body movements. My coworkers awkwardly laughed then relaxed and started to buzz about how we would celebrate that year.

Creativity Doodle

2. Describe the most uninhibited person you know. How does this help them be more creative? Then draw a symbol that will help you remember to be playful.

David, the school principal:
To earn respect from students he relates to them in creative, uninhibited ways. For example, by mounting a desk onto the front of a bike and riding it through the halls. He doesn't care if they laugh or poke fun at him because he knows they are paying attention and find him to be accessible and present.

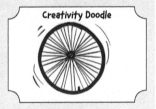

Creativity Doodle

References

Admin. 2015. "How to Think Creatively?" Diplo Learning Corner, March 28. diplolearn.org/2015/03/28/how-to-think-creatively.

ATD (Association for Talent Development) and Rothwell & Associates. 2015. *Building a Talent Development Structure Without Borders.* Alexandria, VA: ATD Press.

Baker, C. 2014. "How to Regain a Sense of Childlike Wonder." WellBeing, March 10. wellbeing.com.au/mind-spirit/mind/second-childhood.html.

Blaschka, A. 2019. "The Number One Soft Skill Employers Seek." February, 28. forbes.com/sites/amyblaschka/2019/02/28/the-number -one-soft-skill-employers-seek-and-five-ways-top-leaders-say-to -cultivate-yours/?sh=644918353d9a.

Brown, T. 2008. "Tales of Creativity and Play." TED Talk, May. ted.com/talks/tim_brown_tales_of_creativity_and_play?language=en.

Campbell, J. 2004. *The Hero With a Thousand Faces.* Princeton, NJ: Princeton University Press.

Chandler, M., et al., 2019. "LinkedIn Global Talent Trends." LinkedIn Talent Solutions. business.linkedin.com/content/dam/me/business /en-us/talent-solutions/resources/pdfs/global-talent-trends-2019.pdf.

Clear, J. 2018. *Atomic Habits: An Easy and Proven Way to Build Good Habits and Break Bad Ones.* New York: Avery.

Credit Repair. 2019. "Smarter Than Smart: Nine Goal Strategies for Success." Credit Repair, August 22. creditrepair.com/blog/finance /goal-strategies/#infographic.

Deloitte. 2017. "Soft Skills for Business Success." DeakinCo, May. deakinco .com/uploads/Whitepaper/deloitte-au-economics-deakin-soft-skills -business-success-170517.pdf.

Duarte, D., and N. Tennant-Snyder. 1999. *Mastering Virtual Teams*. San Francisco: Jossey Bass.

Godin, S. 2017. "Let's Stop Calling Them 'Soft Skills'." It's Your Turn blog, January 31. itsyourturnblog.com/lets-stop-calling-them-soft -skills-9cc27eco9ecb.

Goossens, P. 2020. "Opposite Thinking." Board of Innovation, July 8. boardofinnovation.com/tools/opposite-thinking.

Jonze, S., dir. 2002. *Adaptation*. Screenplay by C. Kaufman. Columbia Pictures.

Kaplan, R.S., and D.P. Norton. 2000. "Having Trouble With Your Strategy? Then Map It." *Harvard Business Review*, September 1. hbr.org/2000/09/having-trouble-with-your-strategy-then-map-it.

Orlean, S. 1998. *The Orchid Thief: A True Story of Beauty and Obsession*. New York: Ballantine Books.

PBS Kids. 2020. "PBS Kids Talk About | Curiosity & WONDER!" Video, PBS Kids, June 18, 2020. youtube.com/watch?v=q5jt-eoBKIA.

Ravn, C. 2018. "Childlike Wonder." Video, TEDxUmeå, June 7, 2018. ted.com/talks/caroline_ravn_childlike_wonder.

Shen, X., G. Chick, and H. Zinn. 2014. "Playfulness in Adulthood as a Personality Trait: A Reconceptualization and a New Measurement." *Journal of Leisure Research* 46(1): 58–83.

Susman, G. 2013. " The 21 Greatest Sidekicks in Movie History." *Rolling Stone*, July 2. rollingstone.com/movies/movie-news/the-21-greatest -sidekicks-in-movie-history-101879.

Weick, K. 1995. *Sensemaking in Organisations*. London: Sage.

Whiting, K. 2020. "Top 10 Skills of 2025: The 4 Trends Transforming Your Workplace." World Economic Forum, October. weforum.org/agenda /2020/10/top-10-work-skills-of-tomorrow-how-long-it-takes-to -learn-them.

Wilson, E.O. 2017. *The Origins of Creativity*. New York: Liveright Publishers.

Index

About the Authors

Donna Porter is an experiential architect driven by a mission to develop human beings over performance beings. Guiding others in the journey to becoming courageous leaders who own their responsibility in humanizing the employee experience is her sweet spot. She lifts up and supports leaders as they lean into curiosity, empathy, and possibility without getting caught up in labels, job titles, organizational politics, and inhuman performance management tactics.

Donna has spent more than 20 years in adult learning and leadership development. Upon completing the Co-Active Professional Coach Training, Donna moved on to obtain an ICF certification. She practices as an independent coach and is part of the BetterUp coaching community. Donna has a master of organization development from Bowling Green State University. She maintains certification in multiple development tools, including The Leadership Circle Profile and Culture Survey, EQ-i 2.0 and EQ 360, CCL's portfolio of Benchmarks 360 Assessments, Four-Sight Thinking Preferences, and Influence Style Indicator.

Donna has organically moved into unique experiences across multiple sectors such as the travel industry, retail sales, banking, hospitality, and higher education. Her most formative experiences were with Council Travel, Sabre, Whirlpool Corporation, the University of Notre Dame, and her business, Marisol Collaborative, where she is the chief exploration officer and owner.

Nancy Tennant is a practitioner, professor, and bestselling author in innovation and leadership. She is one of the world's leading pioneers in transforming businesses to achieve innovation from everyone and everywhere. She is a frequent public speaker to C-level audiences around the world.

Businessweek named Nancy one of the 25 Innovation Champions in the world. She is an adjunct professor of leadership at the University of Chicago Booth School of Business, where she co-founded the innovative and unique Leadership Agility Studio. Nancy is also an instructor at the IDEA Center at the University of Notre Dame, where she co-founded the Innovation Academy, which trains thousands of innovators from across industries, NGOs, and government organizations.

Nancy was the vice president of innovation for Whirlpool Corporation for more than 17 years. In this capacity, she led the transformation of Whirlpool into an innovation powerhouse resulting in acclaim from publications such as *Fast Company* and *Fortune* while creating billions in new revenue. She was also responsible for leadership development and founded Whirlpool University, as well as the affinity group, The Creatives, unleashing underappreciated creatives to find their voice through community.

Nancy has co-authored numerous articles and books, including three bestsellers: *Unleashing Innovation*, *Mastering Virtual Teams*, and *Strategic Innovation*. Her last book, *Transform Your Company for the Innovation Universe*, is a practitioner-to-practitioner, company-focused innovation guide. Nancy's also published the e-learning series, The Innovation Universe Master Class Series.

Nancy has a doctorate from The George Washington University. She is the president emerita of The First Tee of Benton Harbor, a not-for-profit organization that offers life skills to at-risk youth. She is a good, but not great, artist, writer, poet, and lap-swimmer. No matter, she enjoys life to the fullest.